THE
ROCK 'N' ROLL
WAITRESS AT THE
HARD ROCK
CAFE

THE
ROCK 'N' ROLL
WAITRESS AT THE
HARD ROCK CAFE
My Life

Rita Gilligan, MBE

EBURY
PRESS

1 3 5 7 9 10 8 6 4 2

Ebury Press, an imprint of Ebury Publishing
Random House
20 Vauxhall Bridge Road
London SW1V 2SA

Ebury Publishing is part of the Penguin Random House group of companies
whose addresses can be found at global.penguinrandomhouse.co.uk

Copyright © Hard Rock Cafe International (USA), Inc. 2016

Written by Gary Thompson © Hard Rock Cafe International 2016

Rita Gilligan and Gary Thompson have asserted their right to be
identified as the authors of this work in accordance with the Copyright,
Designs and Patents Act 1988

First published by Ebury Press in 2016

www.eburypublishing.co.uk

A CIP catalogue record for this book is available from the British Library

All photographs are from Hard Rock or Rita Gilligan's personal
collection except where otherwise credited

Seminole quotes reported in the *Independent*, Friday, 8 December 2006
Seminole quote in chapter 13 appeared in NYT March 10, 1984

ISBN: 9781785035333

Printed and bound in Great Britain by Clays Ltd, St Ives PLC

Penguin Random House is committed to a sustainable future for our
business, our readers and our planet. This book is made from
Forest Stewartship Council® certified paper.

CONTENTS

Withdrawn from Stock

MY FRIEND, RITA

THROUGHOUT MY FOUR YEARS AS A STUDENT AT HARVARD College from September 1962 to June 1966, I worked as a waiter for 30 hours every week at the Lincoln's Inn Society. Because of my waiting background, I've always been interested in going to new restaurants when they open up to see what they are like from their earliest days. As such my wife, Elizabeth, and I went to the Hard Rock Cafe for lunch on its first Saturday—17 June 1971. We sat at the food bar and were served by a lady named Rita; I said to Elizabeth that Rita is one of the most impressive waiters and restaurant professionals I've ever seen in all my years in the business. I also said that I think that the Hard Rock Cafe will be a phenomenal success in London and all around the world—inspired and led by the one and only Rita Gilligan. My first visit's predictions were completely accurate and throughout the last 45 years, Rita has continually helped to establish and enhance the Hard Rock Cafes, Hotels and Casinos around the world that she touches. I have been working in the financial world since the autumn of 1971 and have brought many very important individuals to the Hard Rock in London for lunch or dinner over the years—they have all admired and been exceedingly charmed and impressed by Rita.

Rita is unique in so many ways—she is exceedingly intelligent, remarkably modest, enormously hard working, very loyal, has an extraordinary memory for people's faces, backgrounds and interests, and can relate to a wide range of individuals. I am continually inspired and motivated by Rita and I often say to myself when I am working on various complicated projects—"Come on Frank get with it and try to make this successful as Rita always does the projects she handles so exquisitely!"

Over the years, in her new role as a Cultural Attaché, Rita has been sent to a large number of Hard Rock properties around the world some weeks before they open to train the waiters and waitresses. She motivates and inspires these individuals, who years later still absolutely adore her and are immensely grateful to her for teaching them how to be very successful for the Hard Rock and for themselves. When I mention to various staff at Hard Rocks I visit that I have the fabulous good luck to be a friend of Rita's, they immediately emphasize to me how appreciative they are to her in so many ways—and always will be forever in the future.

Rita is so incredibly effective, gorgeously thoughtful, beautifully kind, extremely considerate, magnificently polite and charming, remarkably charismatic, very clever and usefully practical, and so appealing with her fantastically warm and very special personality. It's a wonderful thrill for virtually everyone who knows her to spend even a few minutes chatting and being around her. Having the gorgeous good fortune to know and be friends with Rita is one of the happiest, most inspiring, widely informative highlights of my entire life. Rita, you rock!

—Frank Shields

My dear friend Frank Shields and I at Pinktober,
The Savoy Hotel, 2013

FOREWORD

AT MY FIRST HARD ROCK GLOBAL MEETING IN 2004 A PETITE redhead bounced over and introduced herself to me. To say she was a fireball of enthusiasm would be an understatement—I had just met the famous Rita Gilligan, Hard Rock's longest serving and dearly loved waitress and global brand ambassador.

I have known Rita for 12 years now. Her lust for life, people and passion for the Hard Rock brand remain infectious.

She is the epitome of our famous brand slogan "Love All, Serve All." In her 45-year career at Hard Rock she has rubbed shoulders with some of the most iconic names in rock history and treats them as well as our customers and most junior servers with the same unaffected kindness.

With her disarming Irish sense of humor and genuine love for people, she lives the truth that there are no strangers, just friends we haven't yet met.

Ladies and Gentlemen, it gives me great pleasure to present Rita Gilligan, MBE, The Rock 'n' Roll Waitress.

—Hamish Dodds, President and CEO,
Hard rock International

1

ROCKING ALL OVER THE WORLD

WHEN I walked through the door of what was to become the first ever Hard Rock Cafe back in 1971, I had no idea that I was about to enter a world of magic. I was starting a lifetime journey that would take me around the world and see me mix with some of the biggest stars on the planet. I was just an ordinary waitress trying to scrape together a few pounds in London to help raise my young family – and boy, that could be hard enough in itself at times!

In my earlier years I'd been a pretty mean dancer when it came to rock 'n' roll, but I didn't know much about the music business. I came from a sleepy part of Ireland where the closest we normally got to wild behavior was sneaking out a carrot from the farmer's field. But there was one thing that I did know about and that was people. I can talk the hind legs off a donkey and my language can be pretty colorful! Somehow this seems to bring the best out in people and I'm good at making customers smile. My parents always taught me that if you treat somebody with respect then you'll be rewarded by the way they treat you in return. It's a philosophy that's always served me well, whether I'm training a novice dishwasher or greeting a global superstar.

When I began my journey, the Hard Rock Cafe wasn't much more than a crazy idea by a pair of bright American hippies who thought they'd try their luck at selling burgers to posh Englishmen. Nobody thought they'd succeed. London was a very different place back then to what it is today. Fast food and loud music? It sounded nuts to me. You simply didn't do that sort of thing in a restaurant back then. The idea of opening a fast food cafe off Park Lane in the shadow of Buckingham Palace seemed like madness.

There were plenty of people in the restaurant industry who thought that the founders of Hard Rock, Isaac Tigrett and Peter Morton, were crazy. I assume that their bank manager thought they were crazy. If I'm honest, even I thought they were a little bit crazy – and I was one of the first people they hired to help chase their dreams. I expected it would last a few short months, but what the hell – they were nice boys and I needed a job!

In fact, they turned out to be a pair of geniuses. In fairness to Peter and Isaac, London was getting dull and it needed a kick up the backside. The arrival of the Hard Rock Cafe turned out to be the shock that the city needed – and it brought a bit of American culture to the grateful customers in the UK.

* * * * *

Now over 40 years later there are Hard Rocks in over 192 locations around the world, including restaurants, hotels, casinos and live music venues. We started with just 46 staff. Today we have almost 40,000 employees and each and every one of them is like a member of my own family. Isaac and Peter are no longer directly involved with the Hard Rock, but their pioneering spirit is still with us. It's been an amazing ride and I can honestly say that when I put on my coat in the morning it's never felt like I am going to work.

To me, life at the Hard Rock has been one long never-ending party with wonderful friends and colleagues. How else would I have been lucky enough to see rock 'n' roll history being made over the years right in front of my eyes? I can still remember the raw excitement of the first-ever live gig at the Hard Rock, when Sir Paul McCartney performed with his lovely first wife Linda and Wings (and believe me, even though he was brilliant some of it seemed very raw and loud to my ears!). There was the thrill of meeting my idols from the big screen, like Paul Newman and Tony Curtis (who loved a secret swig of the fiery homemade Irish spirit that I used to sneak to him disguised as Holy Water). Then there was the magic moment when Eric Clapton asked Isaac to hang his guitar above his favorite place at the bar, which drove Pete Townshend insanely jealous.

Pretty soon, serving the rich and famous alongside regular customers became almost an everyday occurrence as word began to spread about the food and the fun at Hard Rock Cafe. It didn't matter if you were a superstar or the ordinary man in the street: we treated everybody with the same respect.

By the time the '80s arrived we were ready to conquer the world. Isaac and our original general manager, Prab Nallamilli, asked me to fly to New York to train staff for the first Hard Rock to open its doors in the Big Apple. Restaurants soon followed in big cities like Dallas and Boston. By using that same great recipe for success that we discovered in London, the business began to mushroom until it seemed like there was a Hard Rock in every major city. We never let it go to our heads and we always made sure we put something back into the community by launching charitable programs to help those less fortunate than ourselves.

On the eve of our 25th anniversary in 1996, I was asked to become a cultural ambassador for the Hard Rock. It meant that I gave up my role as a waitress, although I'm still never happier than when I'm chatting with happy customers on a restaurant floor. Two years after taking on my new job, Buckingham Palace announced that I was to receive an honorary MBE (Member of the Most Excellent Order of the British Empire for services to the UK tourism industry). It made me very proud, because in my mind it was the Royal seal of approval for everything that we've worked so hard to achieve at the Hard Rock.

Nowadays, I still travel all over the world to visit our venues in places as far flung as Africa, the Middle East and Australia.

My memories are priceless.

I've met Royalty and I've rubbed shoulders with the likes of The Beatles and The Rolling Stones. I've also had the pleasure of welcoming great American musicians onstage, such as Bruce Springsteen when he performed at Hard Rock Calling in London. But believe it or not, for me it's never just been about the stars: it's about doing a job that makes people happy. Hospitality is personality. Like most journeys there have been highs and lows – but I'll let you into a secret: I'm still just an ordinary waitress at heart.

My name is Rita Gilligan and this is my story...

2

SONGS AND SANDALS: MY EARLY LIFE IN IRELAND

WHEN I think back to my childhood it seems like a million miles from the craziness of life at the Hard Rock. I often wonder what people would have thought back then if they could see me today when I celebrate opening a new restaurant by smashing a guitar with a famous musician. My job at Hard Rock Cafe has given me the privilege of travelling across continents, but my story begins in another world.

The pace of life was very different when I was a child. I grew up in Galway, a beautiful little city on the west coast of Ireland, bordered by endless green farmland to the east. The city nestles at the toe of Lough Corrib beyond which stretch the lands of Connemara to the north, where the country folk live. In those parts they still drink delicious cool water from open wells to this day. Our summers were warm and glorious and they seemed to go on for forever, but in the winter an icy wind would blow in from the Atlantic, bringing a blanket of snow. Thankfully we always had a big open fire at home to keep us warm. We'd use it to cook too, sticking a fork into the flames with a potato on the end or a piece of bread to toast. There were occasionally days when there wasn't much to eat and the food was simple and basic – but to us those home cooked treats seemed like a banquet. My sisters and I would snuggle up in front of the fire and it seemed like we didn't have a worry in the world, although like everybody else we occasionally faced times that were tough.

The rules that we lived by were very strict and the Catholic Church dominated our lives. The Bishop had ordered that no dancing was allowed on a Saturday night in case we failed to attend mass on a Sunday. I went to a convent school where the nuns ruled with a rod of iron (which I'll tell you more about later). Rock 'n' Roll wasn't something that would have been welcomed with open arms by the Church in Galway.

I was born on June 8th 1941 with bright red hair. My father was a kind man called Martin, affectionately known as 'Banjo.' I don't know where the nickname came from. He didn't play the banjo although he did sing, so perhaps it was because he was always entertaining everybody by bursting into song. My mother's name was Cecelia and together they were wonderful parents. I was the second youngest of five children and I enjoyed a delightful childhood. My older siblings were my brother Michael (who's sadly passed away now) and my sisters Maureen and Ann. My younger sister, Martina, arrived a few years later than the rest of us and I can still recall when she was born. In those days babies were delivered at home and I can picture the midwife, who was called Nurse O'Flynn, coming to our house. I was excited because we'd been told a baby was on the way, but we didn't have a clue how it would arrive!

I was aged about 10 and I was getting ready for school when Nurse O'Flynn knocked at the door. She was carrying a little brown leather case and when my father let her into our council house she went straight upstairs to see my mother.

"Is the new baby in the case?" I asked my father excitedly, as Nurse O'Flynn walked by.

My father looked at me thoughtfully for a moment and nodded: 'Yes.'

He was a wonderful gentleman and he wanted to protect our innocence. I grew up believing that babies were dropped off at the house in a case!

My father worked on the roads for the local council. He used to drive a big steamroller that would flatten the road surface and it must have been hard, heavy work.

"Rita, when you are older never stay in a job too long," he used to say to me, but he drove that steamroller for nearly 50 years!

He used to cycle over 50 miles on a rickety old bike to work in Clifden. It took him so long that during the week he would stay overnight in a caravan, so we mainly saw him at weekends. He wasn't a big drinker but he enjoyed the odd pint of Guinness when he'd sing folk songs for us. My brother Michael was wonderful at playing the trumpet and my mother could play the accordion. I never took up a musical instrument, but as I grew older I loved to dance and sing. Today, I'll happily stay up till the early hours belting out some good Irish songs in the pub! I'm a real night owl and even as a youngster I always wanted to play outside until it was late. We didn't have television in those days but we had a radio in the house. It would be a real novelty if we ever got to hear the music show *Top of The Pops* – because my father would usually tune into another station to hear a bit of news and sport. One of my father's biggest passions in life was following the hurling (an Irish game that's a bit like a cross between hockey and baseball). When he wasn't singing he was quiet and thoughtful and he was an old-fashioned supporter of the Irish republican movement.

When you walked into our house the atmosphere was warm and friendly. We had a big table in the front room with a big stove and a giant beige couch for us to sit on. My mother was very reserved and would rarely invite guests into the home. She was a discreet person and would never join in if somebody were to gossip about others. She hated bad language. If she were alive today I'd be hung, drawn and quartered for turning the air blue, like I sometimes do at the Hard Rock!

My mother wouldn't allow a deck of cards into the house (the Church wouldn't have approved). If ever any of us said anything disrespectful she would get her religious statues down from the shelf and pray for forgiveness.

My mother was very caring and she knew all the old remedies and medicines that had been passed down through the generations. My two older sisters and I shared a bed together and we slept in the same room as my mother and father. We had a big horsehair mattress and I always seemed to get the bit that had a hole in it, which would make me itch! My brother Michael, who had a special place in the family as the only son, slept in the box room.

I was born during the Second World War, which meant that food was sometimes in short supply. My mother would get maybe half a pound of butter to last us all week and a good deal of it would go to my brother. He was the apple of my mother's eye and that was very much how it was in Ireland in those days. The eldest son was the future head of the family so he would be given special treatment. We didn't mind – there was plenty more love to go round!

My parents taught me the value of good manners and that was important to me. Manners can carry you a long way in life and they have always served me well, especially when working at the Hard Rock. A lot of my job today involves meeting and greeting CEOs or famous people, but I treat everybody with the same respect, regardless of their station in life. If somebody is rude to me I'll happily give them a tongue-lashing to put them in their place, but generally I like to get along with people. When I was a child, if I saw the milkman or the coalman coming to the house I was always extremely polite.

"Good morning, Sir!" I would say.

Another thing that my parents encouraged me to do was to speak up for myself.

"Rita – if there's something that you don't understand then you should always ask a question," my father told me.

It was good advice. We weren't wealthy, but we were rich in happiness. Most of the clothes that we wore were handed down by previous generations, but every year my sisters and I would be given a special treat at Easter. Our parents would buy us a brand new pair of Clarks sandals. It was like winning the lottery! I can still feel the tingle of excitement when I stepped outside to wear them for the first time. I couldn't wait to show them off. It felt as if the whole neighborhood was looking at my feet! We lived in a very close-knit community in a part of Galway called Bohermore (where I still have an apartment today). The houses were arranged in four terraces where 200 different families lived (I was born at No 35 St Finbarr's Terrace). During the summer the children would go out early in the morning and play outside all day until dusk. It was very safe. Christmas was always a special time but it wasn't the big commercial event that it is today and we'd mainly just be given an orange or an apple to celebrate, or maybe even a doll or a book. If somebody received a special gift then news of it would travel around the streets like wildfire. I remember one year, one of our neighbors was given a *Rupert The Bear Annual,* which caused great excitement and the book was later passed around the whole estate!

* * * * * *

WHEN I was about five or six years old I became very ill and it led to an experience that will cause me sadness for the rest of my life. Like all families, we would occasionally be unwell but usually it was nothing more than a few sniffles in winter.

Unfortunately this was far more serious.

It began when red blotches appeared on my skin that made me feel itchy and sore, as if I had sunburn. I can remember feeling hot and sweaty and at some point my mother moved me into her own bed instead of the one that I shared with my sisters. This was something she would only do if any of us were very unwell, so I knew that she was very concerned about me.

What happened next is a bit of a blur, but I can remember tossing and turning while I was burning up. I felt terrible and I was worried I was going to be violently sick. I was confused and disorientated. I didn't know it at the time, but I was in a fever and I began to have hallucinations. When I looked up I saw shapes of dark animals coming out of the walls. They were big, strange-looking creatures the size of elephants – and I was soon raving aloud in fear.

"Mum! Mum! There are animals in the room, please get them away," I shouted to my mother.

"It's okay, Rita. It is okay. There's nothing there, you're safe," my mother told me. She did her best to soothe me, but she must have been filled with dread when she recognized the symptoms.

I had scarlet fever, which was often fatal in those days before antibiotics. I must have become extremely ill because I was taken away by ambulance to hospital, where I spent many months getting better. My mother hated the idea of me going in an ambulance because it would have been the talk of the neighborhood.

"Oh, did you see Mrs. Ryan's daughter was taken to hospital?" the local gossips would say.

Illness was wrongly seen as something shameful and I felt as if I were being taken to a dungeon. The hospital was somewhere that you would be afraid to go as a child – not least because it meant that you might never come home. It wasn't like today, when kindly doctors sit down and explain everything to you and your family. The nurses wore big veils and patients did as they were told. The doctor's word was final.

I began to recover once I was there, but it was a slow journey made harder by the fact that my mother wasn't allowed to visit me. Family members were forbidden. I was on a small ward with other children to keep me company, but I missed my mother terribly. Thankfully, she soon managed to find a way around the rules. There was a tiny window set high in the wall near my bed. I couldn't see out of it, but it let in a bit of daylight and occasionally I could hear the birds singing outside. Then one day I heard a tapping on the glass, followed by a voice I recognized.

"Rita! Rita! I have brought you a treat!"

It was my mother and she had to stand on a rock outside in order to be able to peer inside through the high window, bless her.

"Take this," she said, passing down a package to me.

It was a two-pound jar of fruit jam.

"Put a spoonful of this into your tea and it will sweeten it up," she explained with a smile.

Those words were so comforting. The love and devotion that she showed me still makes me tearful when I think about it today. Sugar was very scarce so jam was the next best thing to sweeten tea. The jam gave me a boost, but all the tiny seeds floated to the top of the cup (which put me off adding anything to my tea in later life).

While I was in hospital I made friends with a dark-haired girl, who I'll call 'Josie'. She was a young girl about the same age as me and we would chat together and we became close. I was in a normal hospital bed but Josie was given an old-fashioned cot with metal bars on it. When I do charity work today with the Hard Rock I occasionally visit hospitals in poor parts of Africa – and sometimes I see cots that remind me of the one that Josie was in. She was a very troubled girl and she was always unhappy because she was so sick. I'd call out to comfort her, but she would sit opposite me in her cot and bang her head on the bars, moaning in pain. She had meningitis, which like scarlet fever is very contagious.

"You'll be alright! You'll be alright!" I used to say to her.

Then one morning when I awoke it was very quiet. I looked over at Josie and I could see she was very still.

"Hiya Josie! How are you this morning," I called out.

Silence.

"Josie, wake up! It's me Rita," I said, thinking that she was asleep.

She looked so still. Then somebody came into the room – I can't remember if it was a doctor or a nurse – and they must have gently explained to me that Josie had passed away in the night. I found it hard to take in what they were saying. The strange thing was that they left her there in the cot for a long time afterwards before they took her body away. I guess they must have had more urgent things to attend to. It was very sad – I just sat there staring at her and feeling very sad and confused by what had just happened.

I was the lucky one: I got to go home, but I sometimes still say a little prayer for that poor girl today.

3

SERVICE WITH A SMILE

IF you'd told me when I was a child that one day I would have
the confidence to greet royalty I would never have believed you
because I was very shy when I was growing up. I'm a lot wilder and
bubblier today and it's always a pleasure to welcome customers
to the Hard Rock. When somebody visits one of our restaurants
it's like they're stepping into my own home and I welcome them
like an old friend. Sometimes I can even be a little cheeky with
people, but that's just my way. I was at a Hard Rock event a few
years ago when somebody told me that Prince Harry was in the
room. He's got red hair like me and I was determined to say hello
so I walked up and patted him on the shoulder. He was sat at
a long table next to the singer Tom Jones, who I've met many
times and he always gives me a great big hug. Prince Harry was
charming and he didn't mind in the least the fact that I waltzed
up to introduce myself. We chatted for a few moments and I
asked him if he was enjoying himself. He's a lovely young man.

When I was a child, being a redhead meant that I was teased
quite a bit by other children, who used to call me all sorts of names
like 'garnet top' or 'carrot head'. I suppose that today it would be
called bullying, but back then we just took things like that in our
stride. I didn't let it bother me and I always had wonderful cama-
raderie with my school friends. When I was eight or nine I would

walk across two big fields to get to school and my mother would give me bread and jam to take with me for my lunch. It was white bread from the shop, but a lot of my friends' parents were country people and they would bake their own currant cake. My friends would be dying to taste the white bread so I'd swap it for some cake, which was equally delicious. The fields we walked through were full of carrots and parsnips. Sometimes if the farmer wasn't around we'd pull up a carrot and wipe off the muck before eating it there and then, straight from the ground!

Unfortunately, my time inside the school itself was far from happy.

In fact, I hated it. I went to a convent school that was ruled by the nuns and they were terribly strict, you know. They could be very cruel. The school building is still there today but it looks like a big old church. I started going there after I recovered from scarlet fever and to begin with my mother would walk me there every morning. We'd pass a shop that sold four biscuits for a penny and sometimes my mother would buy me some for later. I would get a sick feeling in my stomach during the journey because I was so nervous. We had to cross into a narrow entrance and as we turned the corner the dreadful pains would just start. In school we had a break during the morning and I used to eat the biscuits to try and distract myself from the nervousness. Then at 12 o'clock every day the nuns would make us walk through a dark tunnel under the road to get to some gardens where we would say prayers. They would tell us stories in the tunnel about all the old sisters who had died in the nunnery over the years and I would be very frightened. We also lived in fear of a visit from the dental nurse. If you had a pain in your tooth she would come in and shove a great big needle in your mouth and pull it out. When I look back they were ruthless and horrible. If we misbehaved we'd be slapped across the palm of our hand with a cane – and given extra blows if we dared to move the hand away.

Every month the sisters would make a collection to send money to help poor babies in Africa. Every child was expected to give one penny and there would be hell to face if you didn't have it. My mother would wait for my father's paycheck to come in each week and sometimes on the day before it arrived we'd have nothing in the house apart from a bit of bread and some potatoes. The nuns' collection was always on the last Thursday of the month, the day on which father's paycheck would normally arrive. There was one week when it was late coming and as I walked to school I knew there would be trouble.

"Have you got the penny for the babies," the nun said to me sternly.

"My mother doesn't have it," I pleaded, my voice full of fear and terror.

"Well go and get it! Get out and don't come back until you have it," she roared.

The nun made me leave there and then. I was in tears by now and I didn't know what to do because I knew there was no money at home. It was pouring with rain and I got soaked to the skin. While I was walking along I saw a kindly woman who knew my mother and she asked me why I was crying.

"The sister wants a penny but my mother hasn't got it. I'll have to go back there later and tell her again that we don't have it," I sobbed.

The woman took pity on me because she could see how upset I was.

"Here – take this," she said, handing me a penny.

I trudged back to the school, hoping that everything would now be okay but when I handed the nun the penny it sent her into a fury.

"You see! You found it when you needed to," she bellowed.

And with that she grabbed a broom and hit me across the back with such force that it broke the handle. At first I was too shocked to feel the pain – I couldn't believe that she'd broken the brush on my back. I spent the rest of the day sobbing but I was too terrified to tell my mother what had happened. I was worried that if she went up to the school it would only make things worse. All the other children knew about the beating and word soon spread when they told their parents. A neighbor got to hear about it and she told my mother, who took me aside.

"Now Rita, did she hit you? Did she?" my mother asked.

At first I denied it but when I told the truth my mother went to see the nuns to complain. After that she tried to put me into a different school in Claddagh in the middle of Galway but they wouldn't take me. They said it was because the school term had already started, but secretly I think it was because they didn't want to upset the nuns. The Church was very powerful and they would have been going up against them if they took me in.

I had to go back to the convent school, which I continued to hate, but thankfully there were no more beatings and happier times lay ahead.

* * * * *

THERE were two factories in Galway: a china factory and a hat factory, and when you left school you were expected to work in one or the other. I sometimes thought about becoming a nurse, but waitressing wasn't something that I considered at the time. I'd had small jobs while I was growing up that paid pocket money that I would give to my mother towards the home. When I was aged about 12, I used to walk across the fields to milk the cows in the morning for a few pennies. In those days we used to drink the milk while it was still hot from the cow. I would put the milk in a big churn. People would leave a can outside their house that I would fill from the churn using a scoop.

I left school a week before my 14th birthday and I went to technical college for a year. I was meant to be studying 'domestic science' – that's cooking to you and me! I didn't learn a great deal, so I left and tried to get into the hat factory. That didn't work out so I went to the china company, where I got a job decorating plates. Unfortunately the fumes from the paint made me feel sick in my stomach and I had to leave, so I ended up walking around the town and knocking on doors to ask for work. You had to get a job to survive; there was no welfare system to fall back on in those days. One of the places I decided to try was the Great Southern Hotel in the middle of Galway. It's a very stern looking building made of pale stone and it's still there today (it's called Hotel Meyrick nowadays).

"Good morning. Any jobs?" I asked the bloke on the door.

"Where are you from?" he barked back.

"Bohermore," I said.

"We've no work for you here."

He clearly didn't like the sound of my accent, but I was used to being knocked back and I was determined not to give up. I waited until he was distracted and I sneaked inside. I saw a kindly looking man in a bow tie who looked like he was the manager.

"Please," I pleaded. "I will do anything, just give me a job?"

He looked at me thoughtfully.

"Come back tomorrow morning at six o'clock," he said.

The next day I was there bright and early.

"You're in the dish room," I was told.

I was shown into a big room with a huge sink, three or four times the size of a bath. There was an old lady there – Mrs. McGee – who was already scrubbing and cleaning. There was a big machine on one side of the room full of ball bearings that were used to shine the teapots, which came out battered and twisted but gleaming clean. It was a fine hotel and all the cutlery was made of solid silver, which needed to be hand-polished twice a week. Meanwhile, the plates would be piling up in high stacks also needing to be washed by hand. I didn't mind the hard work one bit, but some of the staff looked down on me as if I was a skivvy. Looking back, the Irish way of doing things was very different from the American culture that I would later experience at the Hard Rock, where you are encouraged to voice your opinion. In Ireland, you had to know your place and you did as you were told.

Having a job meant that I could afford to save a shilling here and there to go dancing, which was the big passion of my teenage years. I loved being on the dance floor. God it was wonderful! I would dance the night away. My friends and I used to go to two big dance halls in Galway, called The Hanger and The Seapoint. We went every Thursday and Friday. The women would all line up on one side of the hall in their big dresses and bouffant hair, waiting for the men. The fellas would come slightly later after the pubs closed and they would line up on the opposite side. The dancing would go on until about half past midnight and to me it felt like heaven on Earth!

I was happy at the Great Southern, but I did briefly leave my job to spend some time in Manchester, England with my sister Ann (who'd gone there in search of a job). It didn't work out so we returned to Galway and I went back to see the man in the bow tie who had originally hired me, Brian Collins. I knew it'd be a tall order for him to re-employ me, so I literally got down on my hands and knees and begged him for my old job back. Brian smiled at me and agreed – and when I got up I cheekily persuaded him to give Ann a job too! We were over the moon with happiness: we had paid jobs and at night we could dance to our hearts content!

I was slowly becoming a young woman and I started to pay more attention to the way that I dressed. When we went out we'd pretend that we were wearing stockings by painting a dark line on the back of our legs to look like a seam. By the end of the night it would be all smudged and wobbly, but we didn't care. Of course, I was still very innocent when it came to men and I knew nothing about sex. The girls at the dances would share gossip with each other about who was dating whom. I didn't know it, but I was about to meet a handsome young man called Noel. He was tall and slim with a mane of blond hair. He was a butcher by trade and he was very shy. I'd caught his eye in the dance hall a few times and I noticed that he had a nice smile. I hoped that he would to ask me to dance, but I got the impression that he had the collywobbles and he was afraid to ask! When he finally plucked up the courage we shared a waltz together. After that, we danced quite a few times over the weeks that followed, but on each occasion he would go back to the other side of the hall afterwards with the other Irishmen, which was the custom at the time.

"Can I buy you a lemonade or an ice cream?" he eventually asked me nervously, after we finished our dance.

I felt like the cat that had got the cream! There was no alcohol on sale in the dance hall but if a fella offered to buy you a glass of lemonade, that was *it* – you'd be hoping to have a sparkler on your finger next! Mostly back then if you met a fella who you got on with you expected to be with him forever, but it was still early days for Noel and I. We became good friends and we'd walk home together after the dances, with me strolling at his side in my bare feet while we chatted under the stars. I adored being with him.

I was living at the Great Southern at the time because my job there came with accommodation. When we arrived at the hotel Noel would give me a fleeting kiss. It would only be tiny peck on the cheek, nothing more.

I was starting to fall in love.

* * * * *

MY hard work at the Great Southern soon paid off. One afternoon I was called aside by Brian Collins, who was still wearing his delightful bow tie.

"Rita, I am putting you in the still room," he told me.

I was ecstatic because this was a big promotion from scrubbing dishes. The still room was next to the main dining hall and it was where all the waiters and waitresses would go to collect their cakes and teas. I was so excited that I ran all the way home to my mother's house to tell her the good news. I was going to be paid 19 shillings a week. It was about 95 pence (about $1.50) in modern money, but it seemed like a small fortune at the time. I was still treated like a skivvy by the waiting staff who would bark orders at me, but it gave me a great opportunity to learn.

On one occasion I got a nasty shock when a chef called John McCarthy sent me to the walk-in fridge to get some butter. When I got there, the door slammed behind me and I was horrified because there were live lobsters crawling around on the floor. Someone had left them there to give me a fright. It scared the hell out of me.

Meanwhile, we weren't allowed to look into the dining room, but during the afternoons it would be empty in there and we would peep around the door.

It was like a palace!

There was a deep, rich red carpet and the tables were covered in brilliant white linen on which glittering silver cutlery was arranged in smart rows. The shine from the knives and forks was dazzling. Everything about the dining room was beautiful. I would stand there trying to imagine what it must be like when it was full of important people from faraway places like America and Europe.

I was about to find out.

The Great Southern must have been happy with my work because they offered to train me as a waitress. I was given a smart uniform that was made up of a double-pleated green dress made from thick linen with a yellow collar and yellow cuffs. It was topped off by a yellow hat and smart yellow apron at the front. I was in my glory! Rita had arrived and I was grinning like a Cheshire cat.

It felt very glamorous and there were several famous people who came to stay at the hotel. This could cause me the odd shock. When the Irish poet and writer Brendan Behan stayed with us for two weeks I took his breakfast on a tray to his room every morning. He would give me a ten-shilling note as a tip (a fortune!), but he made me feel a little nervous, because he had a reputation for being a bit of a character. My tray would be shaking on the way to his room. His wife would be asleep in a single bed next to his, while I placed down the tray. One morning his hand reached out and held my wrist.

"Come on into bed," he said. I wasn't sure if he was joking or not, but I wasn't going to stick around to find out.

"I've got to go to mass! I've got to go to mass!" I yelped, before rushing off.

On another occasion the actor Robert Mitchum walked past me in a corridor on his way to the bathroom. I was a bit surprised because he was wearing a dressing gown and carrying towels. There were no en suite washing facilities in those days, so sometimes you'd see even the most important guests wandering around looking very casual. I can also remember when the actress Elizabeth Taylor came to stay, although I never saw her in person.

It was always exciting to glimpse a famous celebrity, but it was often the ordinary people that I enjoyed chatting to the most. I found my confidence started to build and I began to lose my shyness. I loved meeting new people every day and I always liked talking to them. I was under strict instructions to be polite at all times, but I loved to be able to say a few words to the guests and to make them happy by giving them service with a smile. It's a wonderful feeling when your job involves making people happy.

Working as a waitress was opening up a whole new world of wonder. I'd found something that I loved. It also gave me the confidence to think about trying to find a job in England, where the pay would be better. I decided that it was time to try my luck in London. It was an important decision in my life because it put me on a path that would eventually to lead me to the Hard Rock...

4

LOVE & MARRIAGE: GET ME TO THE CHURCH ON TIME!

I'M a great believer that fate can sometimes turn your life in an unexpected direction. I would never have been lucky enough to join the Hard Rock if I hadn't come to London, but fate also had a few other surprises in store for me there. The biggest of which was meeting my future husband.

I'd thoroughly enjoyed my time as a waitress at The Great Southern and I was still very much in love with Noel, the handsome young butcher whom I'd met in the dance halls. We shared many happy times together and in those days when you were with a fella it tended to last for life. Marriage was never something that we discussed openly but I hoped there was an unspoken understanding between us that one day Noel and I would be man and wife.

My decision to come to England meant it was never to be.

Instead, I met a kind and wonderful man in London called Tony, who became the father of my three beautiful children. Unfortunately, not everything ran smoothly in our marriage but I believe that's where fate also played its hand. Tony has passed away now, but I will always respect him as a husband

and father, although married life turned out very different to how I hoped it would be.

I came to London because waitressing had opened my eyes to the world and I realized that much as I loved Galway, there was a whole planet out there to explore. My initial plan was to come to London for a week or two to see if I could find work. If not I'd return. Of course, this meant being apart from Noel but we kept in touch by letter and we both assumed that we'd link up again at some point. My relationship with Noel had developed into a wonderful romance. If the truth were known, I adored him. At 11 o'clock each morning I would look out of the window of the hotel where I worked in Galway and see him coming down the side of the square at the wheel of his little green van. It was always at roughly the same time of day while he went about his rounds like clockwork.

'Gosh, there he is!' I'd think, while my heart beat a little bit faster and butterflies fluttered in my stomach.

Sometimes during the evenings I would deliberately walk past his house with a friend just so I could feel close to him. He had a neighbor called Mrs. Murray who would point to his window and tell me if he was at home or not. At night I'd lie awake thinking about him.

Noel and I would share trips to the cinema together, where we loved watching cowboy films, especially anything starring the actor Roy Rogers. People would smoke in the cinema and if they didn't have money for cigarettes they'd use rolled up pieces of newspaper. The flames would be flickering while we were trying to watch the film!

Noel was a quiet man and when he wasn't with me he liked to stay at home and play a game of cards with his four brothers. Noel's father had his own butcher's shop and his family also owned a car, a smart black Ford. There were only one or two privately owned cars in the whole of Galway. His family was very well respected and they lived in a part of the city called Shantalla, which would take about 15 minutes to walk to from The Great Southern Hotel. Noel was a real gentleman and I loved the way he spoke to me, so pleasant and kind. He treated me like royalty and always made me feel special wherever we went. I was introduced to his parents and he also met mine. My parents had now moved to a different of Galway called Ballinfoyle. My mother thought he was wonderful.

I was still very naïve about relationships and Noel was very traditional. We would never have considered doing anything improper while we were unmarried, but we'd shared some passionate kisses at the door of the summerhouse at the Great Southern. There was a little corner by the entrance to the door where we could have an intimate moment together. He only had eyes for me and when we were on the dance floor together it was magical. At Christmas he brought me a big decorated box with compartments filled with lovely soaps and talcum powders. It was so beautiful that it took my breath away. It stayed in the house for years afterwards and my mother used it as a sewing box to store all her cotton and needles. To receive a wonderful present like that from a man at Christmas meant so much to me. I hoped that sparkler was on the way!

Noel and I vowed to keep in touch after I came to London. It was only ever meant to be a temporary parting while we saved some money to build a better life for ourselves. I soon got a job as a waitress at a restaurant called the Farmhouse Grill on Edgware Road. I shared a flat with my sister Ann and together we began to discover a new world. London was very different from Galway and I loved the freedom it gave me. There was a big Irish community and the church didn't control things in the same way as it did back home. We were free to go dancing any night of the week and I started to meet new friends. I missed Noel but I was enjoying my new life and I still have many good friends in London, including a lovely lady called Monica Thomas with whom I go to Portobello Road on a Friday whenever we can.

Noel must have loved me very much because after a few months he decided to follow me to England. It was a big step for him because back at home he had a guaranteed job in his family's business, whereas in London he had to find his own way. Thankfully, he found work in a factory in London and we began to see each other again at the dance halls.

Looking back, I think I saw the fact that Noel had come to London as a big commitment from him – so I was a bit taken aback by what happened next. The big event every year back in Ireland was Galway Races in the summer. You would try to save a shilling in a jam jar whenever you could to make it a special time. It was something that you looked forward to all year.

"Rita, I am going back to Galway for the races," Noel told me one day.

"That will be wonderful, I'll travel back with you," I said.

But I was surprised when Noel told me that had other ideas.

"Well…no. I mean that am going back with the lads. It wouldn't be proper for us to travel together, Rita," he said.

Looking back, Noel was probably right. If we'd gone back together as an item that would have sent a message to everyone in Galway that we were formally together. It also wouldn't have been practical to travel together, because Noel would have been with his mates on the boat and they'd have expected him to join them at the bar. He would have been worried about me sitting on my own.

"I don't care about that. I want us to be together," I said.

Noel said that it wasn't going to happen. It was our first tiff and I felt offended. Here was this wonderful man who I hoped would be with me for life, but he was going off alone. With hindsight, I probably made more out of it than I should have done, but, when you are young, your heart can sometimes rule your head. He was a lovely man, but I was hurt and confused because it felt like a snub.

Noel went back to Ireland without me.

* * * * *

LIFE in London continued to be a whirlwind and there was plenty to occupy my thoughts. The atmosphere at the dances was less stuffy than in Galway and it was more acceptable to talk to members of the opposite sex. If somebody asked you to go for a cup of coffee, it didn't mean that you were getting married!

I was at a dance hall one evening when I saw a handsome young man dancing with a slim blonde girl. She was very beautiful, but I noticed that when the man passed by his eyes would glance over at me. That went on for a few weeks. He was always dressed in a very fine suit and his face reminded me a little bit of Elvis Presley. I didn't think too much of it because he was with the blonde girl, but then I noticed that he started to spend time at the dances without her.

Perhaps they've split up, I thought.

It was always the men who approached the women at the dances, but every now and then the band would designate a number as a 'ladies' choice' when the women could ask the fellas to join them. I was there one evening when I spotted the young man in the suit on the other side of the hall.

"The next number is a ladies' choice – so come on girls, pick your partner!" said the announcer.

"That's it – I'm going over to ask him," I said to my friends.

Just as I was about to move I felt a tap on my shoulder and I turned around to see that it was the man in the suit. The fella who I'd spotted on the other side of the dance floor was a different person who looked like his exact double.

"Excuse me, but are you looking for me?" he asked, his eyes sparkling.

His name was Tony and he was charming.

We shared the next dance together and we laughed about the fact that I'd almost approached the wrong man. After our dance he stayed to chat with my friends and I at the bar and it was the start of a new friendship.

Noel eventually returned from the races, but things were never the same between us. I'd been out with his sister Gertie Elwood on the night that I'd asked Tony to dance – and Noel got to hear about it (Gertie is a great friend and she has been a rock to me for over five decades). When Noel heard about Tony he asked me about what had happened.

"Who is the this man called Tony?" Noel asked me, when I eventually bumped into him.

"Well, just somebody who I met," I replied.

Noel wasn't very happy and we drifted further apart after that.

I danced with Tony again and in the weeks that followed we slowly became good friends. He was an Englishman and he was training to be a solicitor at the time, although I wasn't sure what that meant – I just knew it was something to do with the law. Tony was younger than me but he was very eloquent and he could talk knowledgeably for hours on end about any subject. He would tell me all about Winston Churchill, about whom he seemed to know everything. I loved listening to his stories. It felt like I was dating Prince Charles! Tony had perfect manners and he treated me wonderfully, although early in our relationship I discovered that he liked to drink a lot. Most of the time that we spent together would be in a pub, where he would be surrounded by his father and his uncles. It was a new world to me, but I enjoyed being part of it. Tony had asked me on a date after our first dance and he came to meet me outside my home on the following Saturday. He called a cab to take us to the pub and I was a bit surprised when he asked me to pay the fare, but I didn't care because I was happy to be with such a cultured fella!

* * * * *

MY relationship with Tony blossomed and he introduced me to more of his family. His mother was from Northern Ireland and her religion was originally Protestant, whereas Tony's father was a Catholic, so his mum converted. His mum would greet me with a big jolly smile whenever I visited their home. The frying pan would go onto the stove and she'd throw bacon and eggs and everything else into it. She was always cooking and would make great big fry-ups. His mother was wonderfully eccentric and she would bleach her hair in lots of different colors. Tony's father was much quieter and he would sit staring at the television.

Tony was always immaculately dressed and he was a very intelligent man, but I soon learned that his life revolved around booze. When I finished work in the evenings sometimes I would catch the bus home to Kilburn and I would see him and his uncles gathered outside the pub at closing time. He was very kind to me but he seemed to be spending more and more time in the pub. Looking back, the little alarm bells should have been ringing but I didn't hear them – I was too swept up in the whirl-wind of our romance.

We'd been dating just over a year when Tony popped the big question in the pub.

"Rita, shall we get engaged to be married?" he said.

I said yes immediately and we decided to announce it over Christmas. I was so caught up with excitement at the idea of waking up on Christmas morning with a sparkler on my finger that I didn't even pause for breath. I was in love with the idea of being married to Tony and he promised that he would give me an engagement ring at midnight mass on Christmas Eve.

I arrived at the church on the night before Christmas having to pinch myself to believe that it was all really happening. Tony was late and there were only moments left until midnight when he arrived. He was drunk and swaying slightly and at first he couldn't find the ring. He stood there patting his pockets, before he found it in his trousers and handed me the box. Inside there was a diamond ring that he'd bought from a second hand shop for £11 (which was a small fortune back then).

"That's too expensive for her. The girl can't even boil an egg," his mother said later. It wasn't the romantic start that I'd hoped for but I didn't care.

I had my sparkler.

* * * * *

WE were due to be married the following September and I ordered a white dress. Our wedding plans seemed to be plagued by problems from the beginning. Tony was a Protestant, which meant that it was hard for him to wed in a Catholic Church – the only place that my family would have accepted me getting married. Tony didn't want to convert but in the end we found a Catholic priest who compromised by agreeing that he could marry us in the church but at a side altar. I was worried about what my family would think but there was a much bigger shock in store.

Despite living in London for a while by now I continued to remain very innocent about sex. Tony was a fantastic kisser but we had never taken things further. Then something happened in April that would change all that. It was a beautiful spring day over the Easter weekend and Tony and I had been swimming at the public swimming baths with his mother. The three of us were strolling back together when Tony suggested that he'd walk me the rest of the way home while his mum went back to their house to cook. I was staying at a rented apartment with a friend called Betty, an Irish girl that I would later work along-side at the Hard Rock. When we got close to home we bumped into Betty in the street. She explained that our landlady was away for the weekend.

"Why don't you invite Tony up?" Betty said.

Betty had only meant for him to come in for a cup of tea, but when Tony and I went inside we were alone in private. To this day, I still only have a very confused memory about what happened next. I know that I sat on Tony's lap and we kissed...then one thing must have led to another and nature must have taken its course.

To be frank – I don't know what bloody happened!

It might sound a little strange today, but I don't recall making love. You have to remember that I'd grown up thinking that babies were delivered in a nurse's case. Of course I knew a bit more than that by now, but nobody had ever sat down and fully explained the facts of life to me.

A month later I realized that I was pregnant.

I was gripped with fear and terror. It was regarded as filth in those days for an unmarried woman to be expecting a baby. My stomach was filled with dread and I felt as if I couldn't tell anybody, not even Betty who was very religious. I could feel butterflies in my stomach and I had trouble sleeping at night. I was afraid that I'd be forced to cancel my white wedding dress and be shamed into getting married in black. Eventually I plucked up enough courage to tell Tony.

"Tony, I think I am pregnant," I whispered to him.

I will never forget how wonderful and supportive he was to me at that moment. He never flinched from standing by me. He looked at me for a second or two before replying.

"Shall we get married early?" he said.

I prayed that we'd arrange to get to church in time before people started to notice that I was pregnant. I was relieved to have shared my secret but I was still terrified about what the priest would say. I made up a story that we needed to bring the wedding forward to June because my father was unwell (which was a white lie, God forgive me). The priest started back at me in disbelief.

"Rita – will I be marrying two people or three?" he said.

"Two," I said, trying to sound indignant, but the priest had seen through my story.

"Rita, we can send you to a home to give birth," he said. "We will take care of the baby afterwards. Nobody will ever know."

The priest probably thought that he was being kind, but I was horrified at the idea of giving up my child, even though I was terrified of what people would think.

"No, no, no…this is my baby and I am going to keep it," I vowed.

Our wedding day was duly brought forward to June but my emotions were in turmoil the night before the ceremony. I was grateful to Tony for being so kind – he wasn't quite 18 years old at the time so it would have been so easy for him to walk away. Instead he was so caring, but when my family came over from Ireland for the wedding it reminded me of how happy I'd been with Noel in Galway.

I became nervous as I arrived to marry Tony.

"I don't want to go into the church," I said to my father, as I stepped out of the car.

"Musha, girlene!" he said. It was an Irish expression that he used to show surprise. "You've got to go in," he added.

I knew that he was right – and I would have gone ahead regardless of whatever he said. I steeled myself and I walked into church and from that moment on I felt better for the rest of the day. I went ahead and I married Tony. He became my husband for better or worse.

In addition to the baby boy that I was carrying at the time, we were also later blessed with two more beautiful children during our marriage.

And for that I will always be truly grateful.

5

WELCOME TO THE HARD ROCK: 'NO DRUGS OR NUCLEAR WEAPONS!'

IT'S the spring of 1971 and I'm about to walk through the door of what was to become the first Hard Rock Cafe, the one in the heart of London where it all began. I'd come a long way since I learned my trade as a waitress in Ireland and I'd worked for some of London's finest hotels. In those days ordinary people didn't eat out very often, except maybe for a birthday or an anniversary. Fine dining and business lunches were for the wealthy and were usually done in a very formal setting. The world I was about to enter broke all those rules – and I loved every minute of it.

It began with a newspaper advert in the *Evening Standard*.

'Matronly Waitresses Required – must have great personality. Apply to 150 Old Park Lane,' it said (although to be honest I can't recall the exact wording).

What I do remember very clearly was that I was intrigued because the advert asked for older women, which was unusual. The restaurant was looking for waitresses in their late 30s, 40s and 50s. I was aged 29 by now and married with children. I was slightly younger than the advert wanted but I had a family to support, so I decided to apply anyway. I was living in Kilburn in North London, where there's a large Irish community, so I caught a bus to Marble Arch and walked down Park Lane. Job interviews were normally very strict, so you'd make sure you were dressed in your best clothes and you expected to say, 'Yes Sir' and 'No Sir.' At first I couldn't find the right building. I knew the area because many of the hotels where I'd previously worked, like The Hilton and The Inn On The Park (which later became The Four Seasons) were close by. The Dorchester is just around the corner and it's a part of London that has always been very smart and affluent. Buckingham Palace is just a short stroll through Green Park and there are lots of smart restaurants in Mayfair where lawyers and businessmen would meet for their lunches. When I reached Old Park Lane I still wasn't sure if I'd come to the right place. It didn't look anything special. In fact, my first impression was that it was a bit dark and dingy!

I was expecting to be greeted by a man in a tuxedo, which would have been normal back then. Instead there was a young guy stood at the door wearing jeans and an open-necked shirt. I assumed he could have been a dishwasher so I gave him a friendly nod and went past him. He had long hair and I noticed he had a sour expression on his face, he didn't seem very happy.

"Can I help you, ma'am?" he said to me in an American accent.

'Well, I am looking for the manager or the head waiter," I said.

"I am the founder," he replied.

His answer confused me a little bit because I wasn't sure what he meant. I was more used to people calling themselves 'the boss' or the 'governor'.

"What do you mean the founder, what did you find?" I said.

"I own the goddamn place!" he snapped, impatiently.

It wasn't a great start. I hadn't meant to be rude but he wasn't what I'd been expecting. I explained that I had come to apply for a job and he invited me to join him at a table. As I walked inside I found myself in a big room that was empty apart from a few tables in the middle with blue and white plastic covers on them that were decorated in a checkered pattern. There was no rich carpet, just bare floorboards.

When we sat at a table, the man in the jeans turned sideways to me and started to swig from the neck of a beer bottle while we chatted. I was shocked because necking a drink during a job interview wasn't the done thing at the time. He was also smoking a cigarette. This wasn't what I was used to at all.

"Tell me about yourself," he said.

I explained that I had worked in fine dining for 17 years and that I was a great waitress. I'd been fully trained in silver service and I told him that I needed the job. While we were talking I could sense that he was warming to me but there was one problem.

"Rita, how old are you?" he asked.

"I'm 32."

It was white lie, but I'd have said I was 52 if it helped!

"Rita you are great but you are a bit too young. We need older people," he said finally.

I looked at the strange American and realized that he was very young himself. I later found out that he was just 23. What the hell, I thought, I might as well give it my best shot because I've got nothing to lose.

"Listen here," I said. "I am the bloody best you're going to get so you better hire me!"

Thankfully, he found it funny. He laughed as he rocked back in his chair and raised his hand as if to give me a high five.

"Miss Rita, you're hired!"

After that day he always called me 'Miss Rita', never anything else. His name was Peter Morton and he was a brilliant businessman. When I tell this story to mutual friends today they say Peter would never be so informal while hiring someone, but that's the way that I remember it.

* * * * *

THE Hard Rock was very different to anything that I'd experienced up until then. I soon got to meet another young American called Isaac Tigrett, who jointly co-founded the business with Peter Morton. They reason they were seeking to employ older women was because they wanted the restaurant to be like an American diner from the 1950s. If you pulled up at any truck stop in the United States the chances are that a mature waitress would welcome you with a pad in her hand, that was the image they wanted. She might also be chewing gum or have a cigarette dangling from the corner of her mouth – and she'd most likely be full of attitude. Peter and Isaac deliberately went out of their way to hire people who had a strong personality, which is probably why my cheeky outburst at the interview got me the job. That was fine by me, because I was about to learn that *hospitality is personality*.

Isaac and Peter were equal partners, but at times they were as different as chalk and cheese. They looked like a pair of young hippies to me with their long hair and jeans, although I don't mean that disrespectfully because they were both extremely talented. In my opinion, Peter had a very sharp brain for business but he could be quite stern with it at times. Underneath it all he was very likeable.

Meanwhile, Isaac could be very warm and he adopted a more spiritual approach, but he was also a good businessman and he had a great ability to make people feel at home. Together they were a brilliant partnership, although I would later discover that they didn't always see eye to eye.

Peter was born in Chicago and he was the son of a successful restaurateur in the United States called Arnie Morton. Peter's father owned a chain of steak houses and his family was highly respected in the restaurant industry. Peter came to the UK after he graduated from university with a degree in restaurant and hotel management. He'd briefly run his own burger restaurant called the Great American Disaster in London before linking up with Isaac. Peter usually dressed casually but he was always smart with it. A suit jacket would always accompany the jeans and open necked shirt that he wore.

Isaac was 22, a year younger than Peter, and he often wore snakeskin boots and velvet jackets. He was interested in Eastern culture and sometimes after a trip overseas he'd come back wearing flowing white robes. He had piercing blue eyes and he made a big impression when he arrived at the doorway and stood looking around the restaurant.

"Rita, who's that guy in the robes?" customers would ask.

Isaac was born in Jackson, Tennessee, and his father John was a successful businessman. Isaac had attended Centre College in Kentucky but he made money by exporting expensive cars from the UK to the USA. Apparently, it all began when he shipped a Rolls Royce back to his mother and everybody wanted one!

Isaac and Peter had a vision that together they would open the world's first classless restaurant. They wanted it to be a place where a baker could sit alongside a banker or even a billion-aire without anyone feeling awkward. Their motto was '*Love All, Serve All…All Is One*' and those words have become very important to me over the years. (Today the phrase has been shortened to *Love All, Serve All*). Peter and Isaac said that every customer was valuable and that nobody needed to be singled out for special treatment. They told me that this was the reason why the table covers were blue and white – it symbolized a blue-collar worker sitting alongside a white-collar worker. It was a wonderful spirit that a lot of people might take for granted today but that wasn't the way things were in 1971, at least not in London. Restaurants and hotels were very formal. In fact, a lot of Peter and Isaac's plans would have been regarded as crazy back then. Hard Rock customers expected to share a table with strangers if the restaurant was busy, which was unheard of back then. Peter and Isaac also intended to play loud rock music while people were eating.

"Jeez, the customers will go berserk because of all the noise," I thought to myself!

Nobody had ever done anything like that. You could hear a pin drop in most restaurants in Mayfair if it weren't for the fact that the carpets were so deep! Even the new menu at the Hard Rock seemed strange to people in Britain at the time. There was a choice of burgers which customers were encouraged to pick up and eat by hand. Nobody used their fingers when they ate out in England, it was always a knife and fork.

"You'll never sell a burger to an Englishman," was how most people reacted when they heard about the Hard Rock.

The idea of fast food was still new. McDonalds didn't open their first restaurant in London until three years later in 1974, so Peter and Isaac were well ahead of the game. Even the name that they chose was considered unusual. 'Hard Rock Cafe' (there's no 'The' in the official name) trips off the tongue easily today because we're a global brand, but when I told people back then where I was due to start work they'd be puzzled.

"Hard Rock? What does that mean?" they'd ask.

Isaac had apparently come up with the name during a visit to Skid Row in Los Angeles and there was a story that he promised a guy free beer for life for inspiring him. Peter later told me a different story: he said the name was first used on an album by The Doors called Morrison Hotel that came out in 1970.

Maybe it was a mixture of both!

There's also an interesting story about the logo that they chose for the Hard Rock. Isaac was a friend of the celebrity artist Alan Aldridge, who did a lot of work for The Beatles. It was Alan who designed the distinctive yellow and rust emblem that's now famous throughout the world. According to the Hard Rock website today, it was Isaac's idea to model the logo on the design of a Chevrolet car hood ornament (which I guess would have tied in with the American diner theme). But I always thought that the logo looks more like a statue on a Rolls Royce with burger behind it, so perhaps that was part of their intention too!

The walls of their new restaurant were decorated with lots of pennants from different colleges across America. There were also posters of Elvis Presley, which I assume came from Isaac because he was a big fan of The King. Apart from that, there wasn't a lot of rock memorabilia like there is today – that all came along later. To begin with, nobody gave the restaurant much of a chance of being a success.

It seemed too much of a culture shock.

* * * * *

I was looking forward to starting my new job but I must admit that even I was beginning to wonder how long it would last. Isaac hinted to me years later that the lease on the restaurant had been very short and it had only cost around £5,000 (about $8,000), so looking back those first few months must have been touch and go.

Thankfully, Isaac and Peter were determined to make a success of things and they hired lots of other good waitresses. I'd shown the advert in the paper to all my friends, including my former flatmate Betty, who also applied for a job. She was in her 40s and she was slim with long blonde hair. Betty fitted the bill perfectly and after we opened she would actually serve customers while she had a cigarette in her mouth! She'd pause to blow out the smoke while he was taking down a customer's order (this was long before anyone ever thought to ban smoking in restaurants). There was another woman called Myra, who was also from Ireland and she was quite a character. She was in her 50s and she would dye her hair all sorts of different colors, including bright pink. Myra had a fiery temper that she would sometimes unleash on customers but she had a good heart.

Some of the other women had their hair in a big bouffant and wore glasses with a chain hanging down from them, but there were strict rules about the uniform that we wore. It had to be pristine white and we had white shoes with laces, like a nurse would wear. The skirt had to be calf length and we were also told to wear tights – and you were expected to wear light make-up.

When I look back, the waitresses were the people who ran things and it was very clever of Peter and Isaac to let us do that. The founders certainly didn't know everything about how to run a restaurant at this stage but they were always willing to learn from their own staff. In addition to Irish waitresses they also hired a lot of English women who liked to work in posh places. A lot of those ladies were very good at their jobs but they quit in the first few weeks – they hated the loud music and they just couldn't get their heads around the Hard Rock!

* * * * *

WE didn't have a grand opening ceremony; instead Peter and Isaac had a small party on a quiet night during the week, to which they invited a few of their American friends. I'd served several Americans in the past but I wasn't used to their accents. One thing that the girls and I would soon discover was that our American customers would leave us extremely generous tips. I can remember Betty rushing over to me one day full of excitement.

"Look at this – somebody has just left me a tip for ten shillings!" she explained, doing a little jig in delight!

We had recently switched to a new system of decimal money in the UK but 'ten shillings' was the old money phrase that we still used for 50 pence (about $1.25 back then). The going rate for a day's work by a waitress at the Hard Rock was about £1.50 ($3.75), of which we'd normally give 25 pence to a 'busboy' who helped us clear the tables. The tip Betty received was a huge boost to her wages.

The first few weeks were fairly quiet and our customers were mainly American tourists or business people who worked in the area and they came in out of curiosity. Far from being put off by our unusual approach they seemed to like the craziness of the Hard Rock. The food was different but tasty – and we always made sure it arrived at the table piping hot. There was a loudspeaker system that alerted the waitresses whenever an order was ready. My station included a counter area where people who came in on their own would sit. I always had a high turnover of customers because they ate quickly when they were alone. It seemed like my name would be called out loud every five minutes.

"RITA PICK-UP!…RITA PICK-UP!"

Whenever I heard those words I would stop whatever I was doing and go to pick up my plates of food, even if I needed to excuse myself from a customer because I was taking an order. Our biggest seller from day one was our cheeseburger with fries and a bowl of salad, which came with a choice of blue cheese or Thousand Island dressing.

Meanwhile the rock 'n' roll music would be blaring out, just as Peter and Isaac had said it would be – and it was much louder than we play it in our restaurants today. The waitresses would be juggling handfuls of plates and it seemed the faster the music, the faster we'd work. I loved it when they played songs like *Be-Bop-A-Lula* or *Rock Around The Clock* – and whenever we heard *Great Balls of Fire* by Jerry Lee Lewis we raced around at amazing speed!

It was mayhem and sometimes I'd get the orders muddled up. It seemed like everybody got a medium cheeseburger, regardless of what they ordered. Instead of complaining, people seemed to love the madness of it all and it wasn't long before the tips were rolling in. We'd be left 10 pence or 20 pence a time, which would sometimes add up to about £2 or £3 a day – so we could triple our wages if we gave customers great service! In the past, I'd worked in posh restaurants in places like Selfridges, where the average tip would normally be about 5 pence.

Part of the attraction for the customers was that we were encouraged to have conversations with them if they were in the mood to have a friendly banter. Of course, some people would want to be left alone while they ate, but we were allowed to use our own judgment. The staff would gather together each day at about noon just before we opened and we would discuss anything that we needed to know about the day ahead. This meeting was called the 'pre-shift' and it's a custom that has continued to this day at the Hard Rock (although it's now called the 'sound-check'). Isaac and Peter appointed two very good general managers who would brief the staff. One of them was called Nick Smallwood and another was a wonderful man called Prab Nallamilli, whom I'll tell you a lot more about later. Prab went on to become our global Operations Director and I am still good friends with him today.

Occasionally Peter Morton or Isaac would oversee the pre-shift meeting.

"Miss Rita, these are your tables and you are in charge of them," Isaac would tell me.

It was music to my ears. I wanted the best for my customers and I loved the freedom that the Hard Rock gave me to do things my own way. We were encouraged to express our personality to the customers. Isaac and Peter were very clever to bring that part of American culture to the UK just when we needed it the most. We were a showcase for American-style good service and warm hospitality. What I liked most of all was that it was fun. Somebody put a sign up outside the restaurant that read:

'NO DRUGS OR NUCLEAR WEAPONS ALLOWED INSIDE'

That summed it up – because it was a case of almost anything goes, provided we kept the customers happy. It wasn't long before word of our crazy little cafe began to spread. We'd soon be serving movie stars and musicians – and things were about to get a whole lot crazier.

6

GIANT SNAKES & FLYING STEAKS!

WHEN people ask me what it was like to work at the Hard Rock Cafe in the beginning I tell them that it was like going to a wild party every day. I'd been married for seven years by the time I was hired by Peter and Isaac and by then I had two beautiful sons (my daughter arrived a little later). I had a busy household to look after; doing all the cooking and cleaning and making sure my two boys were always ready for school. Once all the chores were done and my boys were safely on their way, I couldn't wait to get out of the house. I'd catch the bus into work, where it seemed as if there would be a new surprise waiting for me every day.

My husband Tony was working as a property surveyor by now, having given up training to be a solicitor, but he still dressed in a formal suit every day. I was also used to seeing men in church wearing a white shirt with a black tie. We had lots of well-dressed businessmen who visited the Hard Rock in those early days, but I was also amazed to greet customers who had long hair and who wore platform shoes and garlands of flowers around their necks. They'd greet each other with high fives and they liked to relax and have fun while they ate. They'd order a round of drinks to enjoy before they had their food, which was strange at the time because people normally had their drinks during their meal. It was a different experience to anything that was on offer elsewhere. There was a rule that you couldn't just have drinks if you were sat at a table (you had to order food to follow due to the terms of our license), but other than that you had the freedom to do as you pleased, so long as you didn't upset the other diners.

We also had a lot of family groups that would visit us, especially during the daytime at weekends. Peter and Isaac were very clear from the beginning that they wanted families to feel comfortable in the restaurant. On Sundays we'd welcome lots of customers from the Jewish community, who would drive down from north London with their families. We had our names embroidered on our uniforms, which was a new idea to us that came from America and it helped to break the ice with the customers. We soon discovered that our diners were made up of a wonderful mixture of tourists, businessmen, families and crazy hippies! During the evening, things would get a little wilder, especially near closing time when groups of young men who'd been out drinking would come in for something to eat. They'd usually be in high spirits and we'd enjoy a good banter with them.

Of course, we sometimes had the odd customer who would take the free and easy atmosphere a bit too far. I was serving in the restaurant during one hot afternoon in the summer when a diner made a complaint that made my blood run icy cold. He was a well-dressed man who was eating out with his family and I could see that he looked very annoyed.

"Rita, there is a snake over there," he complained.

A SNAKE!! I shuddered and his words filled me with dread. Snakes are one of my fears and I started to frantically look around the floor.

"A snake! Where is it, Sir?" I shrieked.

"Over there," the man replied, pointing to another customer who was sat several yards away near the door. "It's a snake – and unless you get it out of here right now I am not paying one penny of my bill."

I looked over to where he was pointing and I couldn't believe my eyes. There was a man in a white T-shirt who looked like he was in his late 20s. He was sat calmly at his table – and around his neck was the biggest snake I have ever seen. It wasn't a little one: it looked like a fat python, and as I watched I saw the thing moving.

"Oh my God! I'll get the manager," I gasped.

I ran to the counter to find the duty manager of the day, who was a young Australian. At first he thought I'd gone crazy.

"Quickly, there's a man with a snake!" I cried.

"Don't be silly, Rita."

"I'm serious, he's over there – I can't go anywhere near it!"

When the manager realized that I wasn't joking he promised to deal with it and he asked the man with the snake to leave immediately. I tried to keep calm but it seemed to take an age for the young fella to get up and go. I had visions that the snake would smell the burgers while I was carrying them and that it would break free and try to crawl up my legs.

"Jesus, if that happens then all hell will break loose," I thought.

To this day I have no idea who the man was and where his exotic pet came from. Thankfully, the creature and its owner eventually departed, but not before we'd all been given a nasty shock.

I don't think I got much of a tip from the other diners that day!

* * * * *

OUR first few months of trading were fairly quiet compared with what was about to hit us. A lot of our English customers were still a bit confused by the menu and they would try to eat the burgers with a knife and fork. The Americans understood it straight away and they weren't shy about picking up their food. They would sometimes be in and out of the restaurant within 20 minutes. Sometimes they'd even eat their desert first to save time while they were waiting for the burger to cook.

"Rita, give me a cheeseburger and a banana split – and I'll take the banana split now," I remember one gentleman told me.

He then sat there and polished off three balls of ice cream with lashings of cream and a banana – and then started his main course! We didn't mind in the least because we wanted a steady flow of happy customers. If people ate quickly and then went away contented it meant there was time to serve somebody else – which meant more takings for the Hard Rock and more tips for the staff. If we opened at noon I'd normally have served four sittings by two o'clock, so we had a very healthy turnover. It wasn't long before we started to see a line of customers outside the restaurant during the day, queuing to come inside. The level of tips that we received was something that Peter Morton kept a close eye on. He liked us to earn good cash because he knew it meant that the customers were happy. The flipside was that if a waitress didn't do so well on the tips then the manager would be asked to keep an eye on her. Sometimes there would be a bit of a pause in business during the late afternoon and the staff would gather near counter for a quiet chat and maybe a bite to eat. If Peter was around he'd come over.

"How are you doing girls, are you making money?" he'd ask. He'd then go down the line asking us how much we'd received in tips that day. If a girl were struggling he'd want to know why.

"We've got the product and we've got a line of customers – you should be making money for yourselves and the company," he'd say.

But actually it wasn't just about the money – by checking the tips it was a way of us making sure the customers were happy. If we worked hard for the customers we were rewarded and we felt good about it.

Peter would normally come in just before noon for a snack and he'd sit at the counter with his head buried inside a great big copy of the Daily Telegraph. The newspaper would be completely covering his face when I went up to greet him.

"Good Morning, Peter – how are you today?" I'd ask.

No answer.

"What would you like to order today, Peter?" I'd persist.

He'd be too interested in the newspaper to hear me but as soon as I went to step away it would rouse him.

"Oh hi, Miss Rita – how are you today?"

"I am fine thank you, what are you ordering?"

We'd then go through exactly the same conversation every day during which Peter would ask me what type of soup was on the memo.

"It's tomato...the same as it is every other day!" I'd say through clenched teeth.

Peter would then order half a bowl, which I'd bring him.

"That's too much, I want half of that amount?" he'd sometimes say.

"Well then you want a QUARTER of a bowl! There is no point in telling me a half when you want a quarter. Don't be messing me about!" I'd say, pretending to be cross.

That would normally get a smile out of him, because he liked his waitresses to stand up to him (Myra sometimes took this a bit to far and I once heard her use some very colorful language to tell him get lost because she was busy).

Isaac meanwhile had plenty of his own eccentric ways that could also drive you crazy, but I grew to love him dearly. Sometimes he'd already be there when we arrived for work in the morning, looking as if he'd been there partying all night long. Occasionally, Isaac would take the pre-shift meeting.

"Open the bar – let's have a party!" he'd say, and we'd all have a quick drink together before throwing open the doors to the customers.

Isaac was a great host and he always seemed to be looking for an excuse to waive a customer's bill, which was known as 'comping.' If it was somebody's birthday or a customer was from a part of the States that he liked he'd be all over them and he'd give them their meal for free.

"Comp them! Comp everybody...everything is on the house!" he'd shout, especially if Peter wasn't around.

It turned out to be a very clever move because it seemed that the more meals Isaac gave away the more customers would fight to come back inside and spend their money!

Prab Nallamilli, our first general manager who I mentioned to you earlier, describes those early days as 'organized chaos.'

"That's why it was so wonderful," he says today. "Even though it looked like chaos to the public, it was quite well organized. We knew how to treat people and what would work. If the customers complained about anything Rita would come back and tell me, and something was done about it."

One of the things that I appreciated most about working at the Hard Rock was that Peter and Isaac valued the views of their staff. If they overheard me suggest to Prab that we could move a table to create more space, they'd want to know more. I'd explain why it would benefit us and then I'd come in the following day and the table would be moved.

"My God, they're listening to me," I'd think.

It was great to know that my voice was being heard. They would also ask how my husband and children were. It was unusual for a boss to enquire about that kind of thing back then, but it made us feel part of a family. It felt like we all had a say in how to run the business and we worked as a team. Peter's big thing was a system known as 'double-checking.' It was drummed into us to double-check everything with the customer.

"Is the food okay today, Sir? Was everything to your liking? Can I get you anything else, Sir?"

Check, check, check.

We also had to make sure the customer was acknowledged within seconds of them sitting down, plus make sure they had iced water in front of them immediately.

Meanwhile, Isaac loved to practice what we called 'southern hospitality.' This was treating customers with the same mixture of warmth and cheekiness that they might have received at a diner in any southern state of America.

"Peter had a great background in business and Isaac was a creative genius," says Prab. "For Isaac it was southern hospitality, for Peter Morton it was double-checking. That was the philosophy of the Hard Rock Cafe. Double-checking: it means whatever you do, go back and make sure you have done it right, whether it be the food, whether it be the service – just take care of things. In both his professional and personal life Elvis Presley adopted the slogan 'TCB – Taking Care of Business'.

"That was our principle," says Prab.

* * * * *

IT didn't take us long to realize that customers loved being part of the organized chaos. They adored it. The kitchen was open-plan and some diners would like to sit on the counter nearby and watch everything go on around them. These customers would often be businessmen who were staying or even living at the grand hotels nearby.

"The food must be nice in a top hotel like that?" I'd ask them.

"It's okay," they'd reply. "But the waiter has got white gloves on and it's all 'Yes Sir' and 'No Sir.' I'd rather come in here and listen to people shouting 'Rita pick-up' and watching the plates go flying by!"

Occasionally, things got a little too crazy. We had a wonderful chef called Benny, who was a small Iranian guy with dark hair. Benny had a heart of gold and he would always slip you a little dish with some chips on to keep you going during the afternoon. But he had a fiery temper and he was very proud of his skill as a chef. In those days, we had a giant T-bone steak on the menu that weighed a pound and three quarters. It was an enormous cut of meat and very few people could tackle it – unless they'd been out for a few drinks, in which case they all wanted one. One evening we were joined by a group of four or five young English lads who'd been out on the town. They were all very hungry and in high spirits after downing plenty of booze.

"I'll have the T-Bone and make it well done," one of them told me.

Benny cooked up the steak in the normal way but after I served it the customer called me back.

"I asked for well done. This steak is not cooked properly," he said.

When I told Benny he wasn't happy. In fact, he'd never had a steak sent back in his life and he was mightily indignant. You didn't do that sort of thing to Benny.

"Who said that? Who? Which one?" he asked, his face turning purple with anger.

"The one in the blue shirt, he just wants it done a bit more," I replied, trying to calm Benny down. For one second I thought he was going to charge into the restaurant to confront the customer. Meanwhile, the lads at the table were having a great time. Looking back, I wonder if they were playing a joke on us. Benny sullenly put the steak back on the grill and when I re-served it to the customer it looked as if it was extremely well done to me.

Unfortunately, the customer wasn't having any of it.

"This is still not cooked enough," he said sternly.

I marched back to the kitchen with the steak for the second time and by now I was shaking at the thought of how Benny might react. It felt like I was facing a firing squad! When I told Benny it was like a small volcano erupting.

"Where is he? Where is he?" he yelled in a fury.

Then he suddenly grabbed the steak in his hands and he flung it across the counter towards the young man.

"Here is your steak – you can do it however you like," he yelled!

I was staggered and watched as the steak flew through the air, causing a couple of people at the counter to duck. Thankfully, all the customers thought it was hilarious. The English lads nearly pissed themselves with laughter and they carried on drinking and listening to the loud music. I served them again in the future after that – and even today over 40 years later it still makes me smile.

It was all very rock 'n' roll and it was only a matter of time before movie stars and musicians started to come along to the Hard Rock to see what all the fuss was about. At first they came in ones and twos and we were told to look after them in the same warm way that we did any other customer (which I think they appreciated a great deal). One of the first actors to visit us was Paul Newman, who was one of the biggest stars in the world at the time, having appeared in big movies like *Cool Hand Luke* and *Butch Cassidy and the Sundance Kid*.

"Paul Newman might be coming in today," we were told at pre-shift.

When lunchtime arrived a handsome young man walked into the restaurant with piercing blue eyes.

"My God, it's really him," I thought.

He was on his own and we left him in peace to read the menu. All the waitresses were very excited and we secretly kept glimpsing over to admire him, hoping that he wouldn't notice. Then 15 minutes later the door opened and his exact double walked in. It turned out the first man, who we thought was Paul Newman, was in fact his look-a-like understudy and it was almost impossible to tell them apart. I had a chuckle because we'd all been swooning over the wrong man!

Another famous customer to visit us in the early days was the rock 'n' roll singer Chuck Berry, who had a lovely smile. He came in with a blonde lady and they wanted to order breakfast. He was very friendly and he spoke in a long drawl.

"We'd like some breakfast, ma'am," he said.

"I'm sorry, but we don't serve breakfast," I replied, shaking with nerves a little.

"Well how about some toast and jam?" he added.

I was about to explain that we didn't have any of that either when I heard Peter call me over to the counter.

"Give him whatever he wants," said Peter, who then suggested that we send somebody up to Harrods to buy the jam. We tried to never say 'no' to a customer, regardless of who they were. Thankfully, Chuck was none the wiser that we had to send a busboy to sprint up the street. When Chuck finished his meal he gave me another great big smile.

"Would you like me to sign this for you, Rita?" he asked, holding up a five-dollar bill that he then autographed and gave to me.

"Thank you, I shall frame this!" I said, taking it and blowing him a kiss.

Soon we were attracting lots of visitors from the world of the rock 'n' roll. Ronnie Wood of The Rolling Stones started to come in to eat with his children and I also served members of

The Beatles, who I'll tell you about in the next chapter. I loved serving them – you could say it was a case of *I Wanna Hold Your Hamburger!*

I think the reason so many famous people appreciated us so much was because we were different to all the formality that surrounded us in that part of London. At Hard Rock Cafe we were a welcome novelty. They loved the refreshing atmosphere. It wasn't like a posh hotel, where you might sit down and stress over what type of knife you were supposed to use first.

Who needed a posh hotel when you could be entertained at the Hard Rock by the giant snakes and flying steaks!

7

PLEASE FEED ME! PAUL MCCARTNEY PLAYS LIVE AT HARD ROCK CAFE

IT started like a normal working day 1973 but I was about to see a piece of rock 'n' roll history being made right in front of my eyes. Hard Rock Cafe is now famous for hosting fantastic live music events around the world – and it all began with a surprise gig by Paul McCartney at our first restaurant in London.

We'd welcomed ex-members of The Beatles to the Hard Rock on several occasions when they came to dine in those early days. The band had split at the end of the 60s but everything they did was still front-page news and their songs from albums like *Please Please Me* and *Sgt. Pepper's Lonely Hearts Club Band* were still on everybody's lips. The first Beatle who I met was Ringo Starr, who came in with his wife Maureen. She was a striking looking woman with jet-black hair, very pale skin and gorgeous dark eyes. I used to joke with her that that her face sometimes looked so pure that it might have been dipped in a bag of flour. She was a wonderfully warm person. She was extremely small and slim and I think she would have been a 'size zero', if such a thing had existed back then.

Maureen was somebody who played a big part in the story of the Hard Rock. She got eventually got divorced from Ringo and years later she married our co-founder Isaac – but all that was still in the future. In the early days she came to the restaurant with Ringo and their three beautiful children, Zak and Jason and their daughter Lee (who wasn't much more than a baby at the time). They were a lovely family and I always found them a pleasure to serve. The children loved it at the Hard Rock. Even when I see those lovely boys today as grown men they still throw their arms around me and give me a great big hug. Zak is now a drummer with The Who and from a very young age he loved anything to do with drums. If you're the son of the drummer from The Beatles then I expect it's in your blood. Zak would sit there as a small boy holding a knife and fork like they were drumsticks and he would bang on the table like a little rock 'n' roll star while he waited for his food!

Ringo and Maureen would occasionally be joined at their table by Paul McCartney and his first wife Linda (who later died from cancer, God rest her). They were also a very friendly couple and were very easy to talk to. Linda was passionate about being a vegetarian (as is Paul) and they would always order a salad, never anything containing meat.

"Why don't you consider putting a veggie burger on the menu?" Linda asked Peter and Isaac one day. After that, Linda created the Hard Rock's veggie burger using her own recipe and it soon became a big hit with our vegetarian customers.

In addition to Ringo and Paul, I can also recall John Lennon coming in with Alan Aldridge (who designed the Hard Rock logo). Lennon was much quieter than the other members of the band and I remember him standing with a tweed cap on his head at the back of the restaurant during a finger-buffet party. He was wearing a pair of dark sunglasses with round lenses and I believe it was the same pair that is now kept in our memorabilia vault at the Hard Rock in London.

George Harrison also dined with us once or twice, but it was mainly Paul and Ringo who were our regular customers. It all sounds very glamorous but looking back it was just something that we took in our stride as waitresses. We were so busy serving food that we didn't really have time to stop and gawp at famous people. We treated the stars in the same chatty manner as we did everybody else and I think that was partly what kept them coming back. They could relax at the Hard Rock without drawing too much attention to themselves, although occasionally there might be a group of American teenagers who'd get excited at the sight of them.

"Wow! Is that Paul McCartney – can you go over and get me a picture?" they'd ask, but we'd politely decline.

We always did our best to try to make sure that the band members and their families weren't disturbed while they were eating. When Paul formed his new band *Wings* with Linda they decided Hard Rock Cafe was the ideal place for them to perform in front of a small audience as a warm up for their national tour in '73. The details were kept very hush-hush in order to avoid the place being swamped by thousands of fans. It was described as 'an impromptu performance' at the time and that's what it felt like. When I went to work that day I had no idea that Paul McCartney would be playing, although our manager, Prab, obviously would have known. There was no pre-shift meeting that day so nobody told us what was about to happen, but when things began to get quiet after the lunchtime rush we soon realized that something unusual was being planned. There was an elevated area on the right hand side of the restaurant as you came through the front door, which we called 'Station One' (it's still there today). I noticed that the tables were being cleared away from there to create a small stage. Word then soon went around the staff that Paul McCartney was going to play that night. I was working a double shift that day which meant that I would be there during the evening. In between serving customers, I watched as Station One was turned into a small stage with microphones and musical instruments, including drums and a keyboard. It was early evening when Paul and Linda arrived for the sound check and they were in a very happy mood. My first thought when they got started was how noisy it was! We were used to tapes of loud music being played but this was different.

"My God! How are we going to work with all this going on?" I joked to my friend Betty.

"Christ! This is enough to wake the dead!" I added.

Paul and Linda were joined by a couple of other band members and pretty soon their performance was in full swing. It was exciting to be present at such a great event, but the funny thing was that we had to keep serving customers at other tables while Paul and Linda were singing their hearts out.

The other diners must have thought it was fantastic; they'd popped in for a burger and they were being personally enter-tained by one of the most famous musicians on the planet. It was great fun but it was also very tiring for Betty and I because we couldn't hear ourselves think. The music was great but the volume was very powerful and raw. After a while, trying to concentrate on our work, we tore up paper napkins and stuffed them in our ears. Soon the other girls did the same and we must have looked quite a sight, racing around the restaurant with arms full of plates and white tissues trailing from our ears like ribbons! Despite the volume, the gig was a big success and at the end of the night Betty and I went up to say hello to Paul.

"Jeez! How do you stand that loud music every day?" Betty cheekily asked him.

Paul just rolled his eyes and gave us a mischievous smile. Thankfully, I don't think he'd noticed the tissue paper earlier, but I'm sure he would have taken it the right way. We were actually very honored to have such a big star choose to play an historic gig with us. It was the start of a long association between Paul McCartney and the Hard Rock, which has endured to this day. I've met Sir Paul (as he is now known) many more times over the years and he's a charming gentleman who always has a kind word to say to me.

* * * * *

THE stars and their guitars have given me some wonderful memories but I also loved serving ordinary customers – and Peter and Isaac were happy to let us have free rein when it came to how we looked after them. It gave me a lot of pleasure to help tourists whenever they came into the restaurant. I'd learn all about what was going on in London so I could tell them where to buy the best cut-price tickets for all the top theatre shows. If Harrods or one of the other big department stores like Selfridges were having a sale then I'd let the customers know. People were always asking for directions to Buckingham Palace and I'd tell them the best way to walk. Our philosophy was that if somebody came to London we wanted him or her to go away and tell all their friends about the amazing place they visited called Hard Rock Cafe. The customers were spending good money with us, so I didn't want them to just go home and say 'I went to London and it rained!' – instead I wanted them to go home with fantastic memories.

We were also very fussy about the quality of the food that we served. We'd sample every dish in the morning and if it wasn't up to scratch or it tasted too salty then it would be off the menu. We never declined a customer's request if it was in our power to help. Chuck Berry wasn't the only person for whom we sent runners up to Harrods! If we ran out of Coca Cola then we'd send out and pay three times as much as we needed to just to keep a customer happy.

Meanwhile, Peter and Isaac treated us well but neither of them was afraid to fire somebody if the need arose. Isaac would come in on a Monday morning and sometimes he would fire one of the managers on the spot if things hadn't gone well over the weekend. If he was around during the pre-shift meeting he'd urge us all to do well that day.

"You see this red-headed mad Irishwoman? She makes more money than I do," he'd joke, while pointing at me!

Isaac loved entertaining in the restaurant and sometimes I'd be called over while he was sat with a big circle of friends who were all chilling out and smoking cigarettes or cigars.

"This is Miss Rita – she's been with us since day one," he'd say, "Come and sit down with us Rita."

"I can't. I've got to look after the tables," I'd say.

"F*** the tables! Let somebody else look after them," he'd reply.

It was all part of the wonderful chaos that made things so special and even within a few days of joining us people would adore working there. There was an English woman in her late 40s who was hired but she was a little bit scatter-brained and on her third day she came rushing over to me.

"Rita, they are going to fire me because I made a mistake," she blurted.

"What did you do?" I asked.

"I gave somebody the wrong bill," she said.

When Peter and Isaac found out they weren't impressed but the woman refused to leave.

"You've got to go, you are fired!" the manager told her.

But the woman wasn't having any of it.

"I love it here and I'm not going anywhere," she said.

The next day she came in to work as usual and after that she just kept on coming in until they decided to keep paying her. Peter and Isaac loved it because it showed the sort of strength of character that they admired. The woman was with us for another five years after that; she just refused to go! The success of the Hard Rock around the world is thanks to our great staff.

Meanwhile, the stars continued to flock to us as word about our crazy way of doing things put us on the map. Sometimes customers would ask for their favorite waitress by name. I always served the actor Tony Curtis whenever he was in town. He was my idol having appeared in shows like The Pretenders with Roger Moore and Tony was always dressed perfectly.

"Where's Rita?" he demanded one day when I was serving someone else.

"Not now Tony – I'm f***ing busy!" I'd joke back.

Tony loved chatting to the staff.

He'd ask me about my early life back in Ireland and I told him all about how my father used to brew his own 'poitín', an alcoholic spirit made from potatoes. It was crystal clear and you'd test it by dropping in a knob of butter. If the butter sizzled it was ready to drink, but you had to be careful to water it down because it was so strong.

"Can you bring me some of that the next time I am in town?" Tony Curtis asked.

I gave it to him in a bottle marked Holy Water and he loved it.

"Rita – one day I am going to make a star out of you," he said (I'm still waiting!).

The British rock band Status Quo were always popping in for a drink and they used to call me 'The Pro' because they said I was so professional! We would also see the occasional Holly-wood A-lister like Jack Nicholson. Meanwhile, I got to know all the members of The Who and it wasn't long before the Hard Rock was *the* place in town to be seen. I can remember Keith Moon, sitting down with Zak Starkey, who was his godson.

Keith told Zak: "One day when I pass away I am going to leave you my drum set."

Zak was thrilled although he would have hated the thought of Keith dying so young. When Keith tragically passed away a few years later he was as good as his word. Zak inherited Keith's 20-piece drum kit that was all white, surrounded by gleaming chrome (years later I phoned Zak and asked him if he wanted to store the drums at the Hard Rock, but he declined).

It wasn't only me who got to know our famous customers. Fiery Myra (my Irish friend with the colorful language) found herself serving the singer Neil Diamond one day. Normally Isaac and Peter would be in at different times of day to each other, but that afternoon they were both sat at the counter together while they watched what was going on in the restaurant. Prab was in charge of the staff and everybody wanted to make sure that Neil and his manager were treated well. They were part of an exuberant group of Americans at a big round table. Myra took their order and Neil's manager asked for a Chef's Salad, a big dish with lots of ham and chicken. The restaurant was very busy at the time and Myra was soon off serving another group of customers.

Suddenly disaster struck.

Neil's manager was fiddling with his salad when he picked something out of it and put it on the table in front of him before slamming a glass upside down over it.

"WAITRESS!" he barked.

"I'll be over in a minute," replied Myra, who was busy elsewhere. When she finished Myra came back over in her own time.

"Yes?" she snapped.

Peter and Isaac must have noticed the kerfuffle and their eyes were now glued on what was happening. Neil Diamond's manager slowly lifted up the glass.

"WHAT'S THIS?" he demanded.

There in front of him was a tiny creature. It was a little salad worm that had somehow got into the dish. Of course, we'd washed our salad, but like any restaurant back in those days there could be the occasional hiccup (don't worry, suppliers are much stricter nowadays!). Myra didn't bat an eyelid.

"Oh, I didn't see that," she said.

Then she calmly picked up the bill from the table and began to write on it.

"Worm-in-salad," she said slowly. 'That's one pound extra!" Silence.

For one agonizing moment you could hear a pin drop while Neil and his party tried to make sense of what Myra had just said. Then, much to the relief of Peter and Isaac, Neil began to roar with laugher and his manager joined in. They couldn't believe Myra's cheek but they loved it. Whenever Neil Diamond was in town after that he always asked for Myra!

8

TAKE TIME TO BE KIND

ONE of my favorite mottos at the Hard Rock has always been *'Take Time To Be Kind.'* For me, it means always being ready to spare a moment to help other people who are less fortunate than yourself, wherever they might live around the world. It is more than just a saying: it's something that we practise on a daily basis. It's a way of doing things that began with our founders back in the 70s and I'm pleased to say that it has remained with us to this day.

Isaac and Peter were both very committed to giving to charity, although they sometimes went about it in very different ways. Isaac has very spiritual beliefs and he became a life-long follower of the Indian holy guru, Sai Baba who inspired his followers to undertake service activities as a means to spiritual advancement. Peter was also a sincere philanthropist, willing to donate time and effort to a needy cause. The money that we made selling cheeseburgers would eventually help to build hospitals for the poor.

Like most rich cities London also has its share of poverty and things were no different back in the 70s. There were many homeless people living down and out on the streets and I would regularly see a group of them on my way home from work. I had to walk through an underpass tunnel near The Hilton in order to catch my bus and they would be there, huddled in the underpass. There would normally be five or six of them including a sad old lady and a man with one arm who used to play the trumpet to raise cash from passers-by. I would sometimes stop to give them any spare food I might have. If I had half a sandwich remaining from my lunch I'd wrap it up and give it to the old lady or the man with one arm. It was my own small way of trying to put something back into the community that had welcomed me so readily when I first arrived from Ireland. I later met the trumpet player in a pub and found out that he actually made a good living from busking! But the old lady always looked so sad and mournful and I wondered about her story and what had brought her to such a situation in life. She'd always have two or three plastic bags with her, which I guessed must have contained her only possessions.

Back at Hard Rock Cafe we'd been open a few months when things took an unexpected twist when I arrived at work. It was a warm summer's day, just past noon and the front doors were open so the sunshine was pouring into the restaurant. Peter had his head buried in his big newspaper as usual and I was standing at the counter beside him when I glimpsed over towards the doors, where something out in the street caught my eye.

It was the old lady from the underpass.

I could see her peering into the restaurant through the open doors, her plastic bags in her hand. She must have been aged at least sixty and her back was slightly humped, God bless her. Inside the restaurant, we had our rock music playing as normal and I think that's what must have caught her attention as she walked by. Peter normally ignored me at this time of day, but he must have noticed the old lady because he put his paper down and spoke to me.

"What does she want?" he asked me, puzzled.

"Well she is probably hungry," I replied, then, without thinking, I added: "Will we feed her?"

To my surprise, Peter agreed. "Yeah," he said quietly, nodding his head, although I never considered that he might actually invite her inside.

So I went out to her and I said: "Ma'am – will you come in and we will feed you? We will give you some food."

The old lady looked at me sadly and shook her head. She didn't say anything but just stood there with her head down. I wasn't sure what to do next and then I had an idea.

"Now you wait there just for a moment," I told her, before going back inside to Peter.

"She won't come in," I told him. "But we could give her a takeaway, you know?"

"Yeah," he said, sounding positive.

Peter then nodded as if he had just made a big decision – and in a way he had, because he had just taken time to be kind and it was the first time I'd seen him do anything like that for a stranger. I realized that despite all his strange ways in the mornings and his occasional grumpy moods, Peter was a good man at heart. The chef prepared a cheeseburger and fries with salad and we decided to include a chocolate milkshake. I had the hot food in a paper bag and I was on my way outside to the old lady with it when Peter stopped me.

"Miss Rita, come here," he said.

When I went over he reached into the cash register and shoved some money into my hand. I didn't count it, but I think there was at least three £1-notes, which was a very good day's wages in the UK back then.

"Oh, thank you. I'll give her this?" I asked.

"Yes," he replied.

The old lady was still waiting outside but she was very hesitant when I approached her again.

"That's for you, ma'am," I said as I gave her the bag – and then I held out the money for her.

At first she didn't want to take it and she just looked at me in confusion.

"Please, that's from us," I insisted.

Eventually she reached out a nervous hand and took the cash from me, before turning around and going on her way. I think she was too shocked to even say thank you, but it didn't matter. Peter had just done a wonderful thing – and to this day I believe that there wasn't another restaurant in Europe back then who would have done the same. Meanwhile Isaac was about to take the Hard Rock's generosity to a whole new level.

They might have been a pair of crazy hippies who could be ruthless when it came to firing people – but Isaac and Peter both proved over the years that they have hearts of gold with their generosity to others and I loved them for it.

* * * * *

IT wasn't long before the Hard Rock was helping the poor on a regular basis. At the end of every shift any leftover food would be bundled up and sent off to a soup kitchen just up the road in Soho, where it would be used to feed homeless people. It was the start of the Hard Rock's policy of helping others that has continued for over 40 years and it still thrives today.

During the early days Isaac would occasionally go to amazing lengths to feed the local population, sometimes throwing open our doors to groups of homeless people. I was serving in the restaurant one Sunday afternoon when he came in at about six o'clock. We were still busy and there was a line of customers waiting to be seated, but Isaac seemed to have other ideas.

"Everybody out – comp all the bills!" he ordered.

The staff looked at him in disbelief but we could see that he was being serious.

"We're closing for a private party," he explained. "Clear the place."

We were instructed to go around the restaurant asking the customers to finish their meals and explaining that their bill was complimentary. If anyone were still waiting for their food we'd wrap it up in a parcel for them to take it away. There were a few people who were a bit bemused but surprisingly nobody complained – it was just another part of the ordered chaos. After the restaurant closed Isaac invited in a group of 10 or 20 people who looked down on their luck. They stood at the bar drinking and having a great time, while most of the staff were allowed to go home. It sounds strange but it was something that he'd occasionally do, particularly at the weekends. I suppose that it was his way of putting something back into the community while having a great party at the same time. It would drive Peter crazy if he got to hear about it, but Isaac would just shrug it off. They didn't always see eye to eye about everything but they needed each other to make things work. They would constantly have different opinions about things like whether or not the blinds on the windows should be kept up or down. Isaac normally wanted them down because he liked shade in the restaurant, whereas Peter preferred the blinds to be up. They agreed that they wanted music to be played because it helped relax the customers (which increased the takings), but given a choice Isaac would normally prefer it louder than Peter.

Our charity work at the Hard Rock is very organized today and one of the ways in which we've been able to help so many needy causes over the years has been through selling our iconic pin badges. If you go on the Hard Rock website you'll see hundreds of different pins, many of which are in aid of charities such as the Red Cross, breast cancer and children's charities. Our pins are one of the things for which the Hard Rock is famous – and people all around the world collect them. The popularity of our pins began almost by accident when I was at wedding party in Soho not long after we opened. Isaac had invited me along with a fellow staff member called Eve, who worked as our cashier. Eve was a wonderful English lady who liked a glass of wine and we were sitting together when Isaac came bounding up to us. He had his hands behind his back as if he was holding a surprise in them and he was looking very pleased with himself.

"I've got something for you girls," he said, with a twinkle in his bright blue eyes.

Then he held his hands in front of him with closed fists.

"Pick a hand," he said.

I tapped one of his fists and when he opened it there was a little plastic button badge inside it. It had the Hard Rock name written on it. When he opened the other hand there was another one for Eve. I was wearing a black suit at the wedding and when I dressed in a smart outfit like that I'd also wear a brooch. I liked the look of the little badge so I took it from Isaac's hand.

"Let's put it on," I thought to myself and I pinned it onto my black top.

Eve took hers and put it on the bar after making a funny face (I think she was too busy enjoying the wine to wear it!) but I liked the idea of wearing the pin, so the next morning when I came into work I wore it again.

Isaac was dating a lovely girl from Texas at the time (this was long before he married Maureen Starkey). I think he asked her to start making a few more of the badges just to see what they looked like. He always gave them to me and I'd wear them on my uniform. I soon discovered that they were a good way of making conversation with the customers. The diners would spot them and ask me questions about them, particularly if they had children, who would always be the first to notice them.

"We love your pin badges! Where can we get one?" they'd ask.

When our first anniversary of trading approached, Isaac and Peter decided to celebrate with a special silver pin, which they commissioned a designer to make. After that we made a pin for every anniversary.

I always wore my pins with pride and as time went on I had dozens of them on my uniform. They other waitresses gave me the nickname 'Heavy Metal' because I wore so many of them.

Every time we open a new restaurant today we celebrate by creating a commemorative pin for our staff. There are also pin badges that are issued to mark special occasions like festivals or major rock events. We also use our pins as a way to help any staff member who may have suffered an illness or loss in their family. We issue a special pin, which raises funds to benefit them or their family.

I've met customers who have giant collections of 20,000 pins and there are over 35,000 different types of pin badges that are listed on various websites. Some of the pins are very valuable and customers in America have told me stories about how they built up vast collections which they later sold to help pay for their children's college fees. I've also met customers who travelled many miles around the world in the hope of buying a particular pin to add to their collection. Each badge is unique and many of them are only available in a particular location. So for example, a London pin to celebrate Christmas will only be sold in London. It's a way for each pin to carry its own little memory of a trip to a particular restaurant or special event.

The story of our pins was another piece of Hard Rock history that I was lucky enough to see unfold in front of my own eyes – and there were plenty more examples to come.

9

STARS AND GUITARS

ONE rock icon who would soon become a familiar face at the bar in the Hard Rock Cafe in London was Eric Clapton. He was in his prime having released *Layla* at the beginning of the 70s and he became good friends with Isaac, who loved nothing more than to while away some time chatting to a great musician. Eric would come into the restaurant mainly during the evenings and if I were working nights I would occasionally glimpse him leaning on the bar in his jean jacket with a drink in his hand. If Isaac wasn't around, Eric would often be alone and he would relax there quietly, enjoying his own company.

Eric has been very open about the fact that in his early days he had a problem with drink and drugs, but I can honestly say that I never saw him looking drunk or stoned. In fact, he always seemed very composed and he was always softly spoken whenever I went over to say hello. I don't remember ever seeing him sit down at a table to eat; he'd only ever be at his favorite spot at the bar. Other musicians would sometimes drop by to join Eric and I can recall seeing him chatting with Bill Wyman, who was with The Rolling Stones at the time (Bill later caused a bit of a kerfuffle by opening his own restaurant called Sticky Fingers, which some people saw as our competition). I also saw Mick Jagger drop by for a drink and

I got used to the fact that it sometimes seemed like we'd be greeting a different star every day. Pete Townshend from The Who was another regular who became good mates with Isaac – and I eventually lost count of the number of musicians who would pop in and out to say hello.

It was around this time that Eric started dating Pattie Boyd, the ex-wife of George Harrison from The Beatles. Pattie was a stunning looking woman and sometimes she'd join Eric at the bar. This was before the Hard Rock was famous for our collection of rock and roll memorabilia, but that was soon about to change, thanks to Eric.

I came into work one morning to discover that we had a new piece of decoration hanging up behind the bar. It was a burgundy electric guitar and it was close to the spot where Eric liked to lean on the bar.

"What do you think? It was a gift from Eric Clapton," Isaac later proudly told us.

The guitar was a classic Fender Lead II and it was the first-ever major item of rock memorabilia to grace our walls – if you don't count Isaac's old posters of Elvis, that is! Today we have a collection of over 74,000 priceless items (some of which I'll tell you about later) but it all began with that red Fender. Apparently, Eric just came in with it one day and handed it over.

I can imagine Isaac saying to Eric: "But I don't play the goddamn guitar!"

Eric apparently told him: "Hang it on the wall. It'll mark my spot."

It didn't take long for word to spread about Eric's gift. About a week later a package arrived at the Hard Rock containing a second guitar and a note.

It said: "Mine's as good as his! Love, Pete."

It was from Pete Townshend. He wasn't going to let Eric steal his thunder without a fight! According to our website today, our memorabilia collection therefore began as "a good ol' fashioned one-upmanship battle between two of rock's greatest guitar players" – and that's exactly how it was!

Both Eric and Pete went on to become long-standing friends of the Hard Rock and over the years that followed we were very honored to welcome them to many events and functions. I've met them both on several occasions and they always have a kind word to say. Eric later founded a treatment center in Antigua for people with addiction problems and the Hard Rock has worked with him on many charity projects.

The story of Eric's guitar became a bit of a rock 'n' roll legend and there's an interesting story about it that occurred many years later. After we'd opened a restaurant in Orlando, we sent the guitar over to be the showcase item in a memorabilia vault that we established in Florida. The guitar was duly stored safely in America for a while, but we later decided to bring it back to its original home in London. To celebrate, Eric kindly agreed to visit the Hard Rock Cafe in order to sign it personally (which he hadn't done first time around). He was also to sign a special T-shirt that we were planning to sell for charity. Eric was rightly regarded as a guitar god all around the world by now – so it was a big occasion for us and I was asked to greet him on the red carpet that morning.

Unfortunately, there was a problem when I arrived.

One of our senior executives was personally bringing the guitar to London in order to keep it safe – but the customs officers at the airport had other ideas for it. They were so intrigued by the guitar that for some reason they took the decision to impound it. It would take several days for all the red tape to be sorted out – and meanwhile there would be no guitar to sign.

"You'll just have to do your best to explain to Eric when he arrives," a colleague told me.

Eric was due very early – I think about 8 o'clock in the morning – and when his car pulled up I stepped onto the carpet to welcome him.

"Hi Eric, welcome back to the Hard Rock," I said.

"Hi Rita, how are you?" he replied.

"I'm fine and I'm still working here as you can see," I said, as we strolled into the restaurant together. When we got inside there was an awkward moment when I had to explain what had happened.

"Where's the guitar?" Eric asked.

"It's been held up at customs," I explained. "They probably thought it was full of drugs!" I joked.

It was an innocent comment and I hadn't meant it disrespectfully because Eric would never do drugs these days. Thankfully Eric laughed out loud and we sat down for a soft drink while he signed the T-shirt for charity. Eric was kind and lovely, but I found the occasion slightly sad because it reminded me of the last time I'd spoken to him in London, which had been shortly before the tragic death of his child Conor.

In the past, Eric's eyes had always lit up whenever he spoke about his son.

"When are you going to bring in the boy to see us?" I'd previously asked him.

Sadly it was never to be, because Conor was killed in a tragic accident at a hotel and Eric wrote the song *Tears From Heaven* about his pain and loss. When he arrived to sign the T-shirt I could sense there was sadness behind his smile. I hope that with the passage of time he's managed to now find peace of mind, but as a parent myself I can only imagine how hard it must be to come to terms with the loss of a child. It doesn't matter who you are in life: it's your loved ones who always matter the most.

* * * * *

OUR Hard Rock staff tend to come from interesting backgrounds, this is something that dates back to the very beginning. As well as all those wonderful early characters like Myra and Benny who I've told you about already, Isaac and Peter also hired lots of family members of famous people over the years. They'd work ordinary jobs like bartending or bussing tables, and they were treated just like any other member of staff. Nobody was given special treatment, but it made life in the restaurant all the more interesting. Among our early recruits was a delightful young man called Rock Brynner. He was the son of the Hollywood icon Yul Brynner, who had starred in hugely successful movies like *The King and I* and *The Magnificent Seven*. Rock was a bubbly character who worked with us as a barman and his father obviously knew everybody in Hollywood.

Another person who joined us a member of staff a bit later on was the daughter of the famous musical composer Andre Previn. Her name was Lovely and she joined us a waitress in the late 70s when she was a fan of punk rock, which was all the rage at the time in London. Another person who I got to know very well was Mick Jagger's younger brother Chris, who used to help out by serving behind the bar.

Our employees also included the sons of the actor Stanley Baker (who starred in *Zulu* and who was also a great drinking friend of Richard Burton). Stanley's sons were lovely boys called Martin and Glyn. Martin worked in the finance office and Glyn worked in the bar and restaurant. Another person from a famous family who worked with us was Zac Goldsmith, who later became an MP (and at the time of writing this book he's in the running to become Mayor of London).

Ringo Starr's children also took various jobs with us when they were old enough to help around the restaurant and they became part of the family, especially when their mum Maureen started to date Isaac after she split from Ringo. When Isaac and Maureen's relationship became public the newspapers got very excited and I can remember reading headlines along the lines of: 'EX BEATLE'S WIFE DATES HARD ROCK CO-FOUNDER!' It all sounded very exciting but looking back we just took it on our stride: it was all just part of everyday life at the Hard Rock.

I was serving in the restaurant one afternoon when a very special guest from America came to join us. I didn't see him arrive: I just looked up and he was there with a large group who'd sat down at a large table on my station. It was the boxer Muhammad Ali, who was heavyweight champion of the world at the time. I don't know much about boxing, but like everybody else I'd watched some of his fights on TV, which were always huge events. Back in the 60s, he'd been known as Cassius Clay, but he'd changed his name to Ali after becoming the champ. He was very flamboyant whenever he appeared on TV and always had lots to say for himself. It was around the time that Ali was due to fight in Dublin and I think Rock Brynner knew members of his entourage. Ali was wearing a smart suit and was very relaxed. He was with several friends and there were also some children in their party. It was lovely to be able to see such a great sportsman at the Hard Rock so I wanted to give him a warm welcome. I went up and put my hand on his shoulder.

"Hello, how are you today?" I asked.

Ali looked up at me with his beautiful eyes.

"Hiiiii," he said.

"You're on my table today, mister. What can I get you?"

I'd seen him in the ring when his attitude was 'Float like a butterfly, sting like a bee', but in the flesh he had a presence about him that was very calm and collected. He spoke softly and slowly and he had very good manners. It was lovely to see him relaxing at what I assume must have been a family occasion. It made my day – after all it's not every day that you get the meet the heavyweight champion of the world!

Another person whom I enjoyed meeting was the actress Joan Collins and her sister, the novelist. They were always immaculately dressed whenever they came into the Hard Rock. Joan was very organized and she sat with her children and a group of friends at the same big round table where Muhammad Ali had chosen to sit.

"We'll only need one menu," she told me. Joan then asked everyone around the table what they wanted and ordered the food on their behalf.

"That's four cheeseburgers for the others please," she said.

"And what about you?" I asked.

"Oh, nothing for me," she said.

Joan always had perfect manners and I served her on numerous occasions after that. Her sister Jackie, R.I.P., was also great fun and she had a wonderful sense of humor. She came in one afternoon with the singer Suzi Quatro and the pair of them were sat chatting when they were spotted by a group of four young English guys who were seated nearby.

"Is that Jackie Collins?" one of the lads asked as I walked by.

"Yes, it is," I replied.

Jackie was very attractive and I could see the guys were very excited.

"We'd like to buy her a bottle of champagne, would you go over and ask if she'll accept it?" one of them asked me.

When I told Jackie she agreed.

"Oh yes, that would be nice," she said.

I was a bit nervous about opening the bottle at the table because I wasn't used to popping the cork, but when I arrived with the bottle Jackie stopped me.

"Don't open it," she said. Jackie then pulled the bottle out of the bucket and gave it a wipe with a tissue. 'Thank you,' she added as she placed it into her bag so that she could take it with her when she left.

The lads opposite thought it was hilarious and didn't mind in the least!

* * * * *

LOOKING back there was always crazy stuff going on – and a lot of great things seemed to happen by accident. Some of our kitchen staff and busboys were keen football players and a few of them got talking and decided to form a team. I didn't pay much attention to it but when Isaac and Peter got to hear about it they decided to kit the lads out in Hard Rock shirts for a game they organized in the park nearby. They were off-white T-shirts with just our name and logo on (they didn't have the word 'London' on them like they do today). I don't know who won the football match but after the game there were four or five spare shirts left over which somebody shoved into a paper bag and put to one side. Back in those days we had a basement, which is now the lower level of our restaurant in Old Park Lane. The T-shirts ended up downstairs in a crumped heap, spilling out of the bag. It was a part of the building that we used for storage in those days and sometimes the cashiers would go down there to count the takings.

Sometimes during the afternoons there would be a quiet spell in the restaurant at around 3 o'clock and group of us might go downstairs to have a chat. We were down there one day when my friend Betty picked up the bag with the football T-shirts inside it.

"What's that?" Peter Morton asked.

Betty explained they were the leftover T-shirts and I could sense Peter's mind ticking over. We got chatting and I think it was Peter's idea to try and sell the T-shirts upstairs. After all, there were plenty of people who probably wanted to show that they'd visited the same restaurant as the likes of Muhammad Ali, Jackie Collins and Paul McCartney. The pin badges that I'd started to wear often caught the eyes of customers, so maybe some of them might also like the idea of a T-shirt? We put the four shirts upstairs under the cashier's desk and occasionally I'd bring them to the attention of customers, particularly any Americans who might want a souvenir of their visit to London.

"Would you like to see any of our merchandise? We have some nice T-shirts for sale today?" I'd say.

"No thanks. We're going to Harrods to look around but we'll come back if we need one," the customers would reply.

At first there wasn't much interest, but slowly the idea caught on and eventually we sold all the shirts. After that Isaac and Peter ordered some more shirts and word began to spread. It wasn't long before we were selling them in huge numbers and today our global merchandising business is worth hundreds of millions of dollars and it has also raised huge sums for charity, thanks to people like Eric Clapton. I'm always amazed when I remember that it all began with that crumpled paper bag down in the basement!

10

IN SICKNESS AND
IN HEALTH

MY work colleagues at the Hard Rock were becoming like a second family who would support me through thick and thin. Everything was going brilliantly at work and by 1975 Hard Rock Cafe had already build up a great reputation around the world, even though London was still our only restaurant at that time. My work gave me freedom and fun and I loved every minute of it. Unfortunately, there were a few shocks in store for me – including a nasty health scare.

I had two beautiful sons at home; John, my eldest and Darren. They were wonderful little boys who have grown up into fine men and I love them dearly. When they were aged eight and nine they were attending separate schools because of their age difference. I had a very busy time at home cooking and cleaning and the mornings were especially busy. I would make the boys breakfast and ensure they were washed and ready for the day. I'd then walk them to their respective schools before dashing back to our house and getting changed into my waitressing uniform. It was hard work, but I didn't mind one little bit.

The only cloud on the horizon was that my relationship with my husband Tony didn't always run as smoothly as I hoped.

He was a wonderful man and we rarely argued, but he continued to be a very heavy drinker. He was very entertaining and he could be wonderful company but the booze always came first. I didn't complain because back in those days the husband was considered the boss. My job at the Hard Rock had opened my eyes to a modern way of doing things, but back home my marriage was very old-fashioned. It had settled into a regular pattern in which Tony spent all his time in pubs and nightclubs and there were many days that went by in which I rarely saw him until he came home in the early hours. Looking back there were times when I felt lonely at home without him, but I had my boys and my pals at the Hard Rock like Betty and Elizabeth, who were always there for me. Betty and I used to drive poor Prab mad in the restaurant because we never stopped chatting to one another. I told you at the beginning of this book that I can talk the hind legs off a donkey and Betty was the same. At the end of our shift we'd share a bus home and we'd spend the whole journey talking some more. Once, when we went off on holiday to different places we ran up a huge phone bill keeping in touch and we had to borrow money from Prab to settle our telephone bills!

Betty was a dear friend who I could confide in, but I hid a lot of my worries about Tony's drinking from everybody. Tony always looked immaculate and nobody looking at him would have guessed that he had a drink problem.

* * * * *

THE difficulties had started early in our marriage. I will always love and respect Tony but he could be very selfish when it came to booze. We had spent our wedding night in the rented room where we lived in North London and the next morning Tony awoke with an appetite.

"What have we got for breakfast?" he asked me.

I think I had some bread and butter in the room but nothing special. Tony got up and went downstairs to our landlady's fridge and helped himself to her bacon and sausages, plus he brought up her morning newspaper. I was shocked.

"You can't do that Tony, you know!"

He just replied: "We have to have breakfast!"

Then he cheerfully ate the lot! After that he got dressed and went to the pub. I can't remember whether or not he invited me along, but I wouldn't have gone to a pub during the day. It wouldn't have been considered a proper thing for a woman to do because he would have been mixing with all the men. He spent the day after our wedding drinking with his mates while I stayed alone in the room, pregnant. I didn't complain because like I say, the husband was the boss in those days. Today I would have plenty to say.

Our landlady was very upset about her missing sausages and she knocked on our door to complain. I didn't know what to say to her. Tony and I went for a short honeymoon in Ireland two days later. When we returned to England we lived in that house in North London for six months. I would cook dinner each night and he would eat it before going out again every night when the pubs opened at 7pm. Then one day I asked him a question.

"Tony, how much do you drink?"

He told me that at weekends he drank about nine or ten pints of beer in the morning and 11 or 12 more at night. Today I know that's an awful lot, but I didn't say anything. He was

18 at the time. Our first Christmas together was very sad, and I still get upset if I think about it today. We were in a pub with Tony's father in West Hampstead on Christmas Eve. I was expecting our first baby and I hoped that we'd be able to enjoy a family Christmas. Tony excused himself for a moment to go to the toilet while we were in the pub and his father chose that moment to speak to me while we alone.

"Tony is coming for Christmas dinner tomorrow at the house. Now you can come if you want, Rita – but you are nothing to us," he said unkindly.

I was speechless.

It was hard not to burst into tears but when Tony came back from the bathroom I didn't say anything. The next morning I knew I wasn't welcome at his family's home.

"Tony, I am not going," I said.

Tony got up and left me without any hesitation. I stayed there stuck in that room alone and pregnant. The baby was showing on my figure by now because I was heavily pregnant. I had nobody to talk to because we didn't have a phone and the landlady wasn't somebody who I could confide in. The only food that I had was bread and jam and I sat there staring out of the window.

"Maybe he'll come back, maybe he'll come back," I said to myself over and over again.

I stayed alone in that room for four days until he returned.

* * * * *

TONY and I had been married for ten years when I received some news that made me happy. I was pregnant again and the new baby was due in January. With two lovely boys already in the family I secretly hoped that the new baby would be a girl. Several of the other waitresses had fallen pregnant during my time at the Hard Rock – so I wondered if there was something healthy in the water! One of the girls who conceived was an Austrian waitress called Maria. Before she told anybody I'd had a premonition that she was expecting – and she was amazed when I asked her.

"How did you know that?" she gasped.

"I just had a funny feeling," I explained.

When it came to announcing my own baby news, Betty, Myra and all the girls were delighted for me. The Hard Rock has always been brilliant at looking after employees and there was never any doubt that Isaac and Peter would agree to hold open my job for me while I took time off to have the baby.

I felt pleased at the thought of another baby to love and care for, but as the weeks ticked away towards January I realized that something inside me was starting to feel a bit wrong. One day I was doing the washing up in the morning and getting ready to take my boys up the road to school when I suddenly burst into tears. I felt very low and I wasn't sure why. After that I found that I'd come home from work at different times of day and start crying. I managed to hide things from my colleagues at work, but away from the Hard Rock I seemed to be constantly low. I'd heard of women being depressed after having a baby, but I was feeling low BEFORE the baby had arrived. I just wasn't my normal self, so I decided to ask the doctor for help and I made an appointment to see him.

"Doctor, I don't know what's wrong. I am just crying all the time."

He listened to me and suggested that I go to a specialist at St Mary's Hospital, where I was seen by a very distinguished consultant called Mr. George Pinker. He was a very kind silvered-haired gentleman who was very well known at the time because he also happened to be gynecologist to The Queen. He also later looked after Princess Diana and he delivered Prince William and Prince Harry – so I was in very good hands. The National Health Service in Britain is a wonderful system and I was very flattered that I got to see the same physicians as royalty. Mr. Pinker sent me for some tests and when the results came back it was bad news.

"I'm afraid you have got fibroids and they are as big as grape-fruits," he said.

I listened in shock as Mr. Pinker gently explained that fibroids are non-cancerous tumors that grow on the ovaries and that they needed to be removed.

"Now, we can terminate the pregnancy..." he said.

"What do you mean 'terminate'?" I asked.

"Abort," he replied.

"Oh no, no, no...I'm Catholic," I stuttered. "I am not aborting the baby."

There was no way I wanted to lose the innocent life that I was carrying inside of me. I decided to have the baby and asked the doctor to postpone the operation until after the child was born.

"Will the baby be alright?" I asked.

"The baby will survive but you are going to suffer after-wards," said Mr. Pinker, who then explained that I would need a hysterectomy, which was a very major operation to go through in those days.

"It doesn't matter about me – the baby comes first," I said.

The hospital monitored me closely throughout the rest of the pregnancy. I went for a check-up one Friday afternoon in January close to the date when the baby was due. The doctors said everything was normal and that they didn't need to see me again over the weekend, but when I got home there was a knock on the door. It was one of the young doctors from the hospital and he was looking flustered.

"Missus Gilligan, you have to come back to the hospital the baby is on the way," he said.

"No that can't be right…I've just come back from there. They told me to stay at home over the weekend," I explained.

"No – we've re-checked the tests and the baby is coming soon," he insisted.

My boys were still at school so I promised the doctor I would go back to the hospital as soon as I could contact Tony to ask him to collect the children. Unfortunately, that was the start of a nightmare. Tony was out drinking and I knew the only way to find him would be to trawl through the pubs. The first one I went to was called The Prince of Wales.

"Is Tony here?" I asked.

"No, he is not."

The place was full of men and I was embarrassed to be in there on my own while I was carrying an unborn baby. I only had enough money on me for one bus fare to the hospital, which meant that I had to search on foot. I eventually found Tony in the fifth pub that I went to. He was drinking with his mates.

"Tony, can you collect the boys from school? I have got to go back to hospital, the baby is one the way," I explained.

I'll never forget his words.

"Rita, I am in company," he said, refusing to leave the pub.

I tried my best to persuade him but I knew that while he had drink inside him it would be impossible to change his mind. I went back home and persuaded two of my neighbors to collect the boys. I went back to the hospital where they said the baby would be delivered the following morning. There was a bit of a delay the next day because the ward was busy. I gave birth at half past ten the following evening, after a long and tiring delivery.

When I cuddled the beautiful baby in my arms for the first time I knew it was all worth it. Holding a new child is a lovely feeling and I was delighted that I had the healthy baby girl that I was hoping for. She was a miracle from God and I called her Tara. She weighed 11 and half pounds.

I was happy and relieved, but there was still no sign of Tony. He had telephoned during the Saturday afternoon from a drinking club, but he didn't come to the hospital. On the Sunday, a big group of my friends from the Hard Rock arrived downstairs at the hospital to congratulate me, but I asked them not to come onto the ward: I wanted Tony to be the first to see the new baby. He didn't come to see me until the following Tuesday when he eventually rocked up very drunk, nearly four days late.

* * * * *

I had the hysterectomy operation a few months after Tara was born. I arranged for Tony's mother to look after my boys and I prepared myself for what lay ahead. Mr. Pinker was wonderful. He had a very special manner with his patients. He also had a mischievous sense of humor. On one occasion he brought a team of junior doctors with him when he came to see me while I was on the hospital ward.

"Mrs. Gilligan is very strong," he told his students. "And I'll tell you why," he added.

Mr. Pinker then opened up my bedside cupboard where he knew I had four cans of Guinness! My mother had sent them to me so that I could sip an inch of stout with some milk to keep my strength up!

In truth, I was very ill after having the baby and I was still crying a lot. The operation was a shock to my system and afterwards I had to take 22 tablets every day while the doctors attempted to make me better. Unfortunately I developed a nasty infection and for a while things seemed to be going from bad to worse. The scar on my stomach was not healing. The doctors explained that I would need to go to a care home to convalesce. I had to choose between a place in Bayswater in London and another place at a sleepy little village in Oxfordshire called Nettlebed. In the end it was Mr. Pinker who made the decision.

"Mrs. Gilligan is not going to Bayswater because she will insist on going out and about there," he said.

He knew that no matter how sick I was, I wouldn't be able to resist a trip to the shops in London! So off I went to Nettlebed where I stayed at a delightful country home called Joyce Grove, which was donated to St Mary's Hospital by the Fleming family. It was where Ian Fleming, the author of the James Bond books, had spent some of his childhood.

There was an elderly white-haired doctor in his 80s who used to visit the home twice a week. He had two little sausage dogs, which he brought along on a leash whenever he arrived. He examined my stomach and knew what to do straight away.

"Take her off all medication," he ordered.

The elderly doctor then instructed the nurses to mix up an old-fashioned poultice using white bread and salt. They gently placed it on my stomach and finally it began to heal. Sometimes the old remedies are the best.

I was off work for about two months while I was recovering from the operation. During that time the Hard Rock and all our staff were a pillar to me. When I finally got better, Isaac and Peter welcomed me home to the Hard Rock with open arms. It had been a long struggle but it was worth it. I was back in the Hard Rock where I belonged – and I had my beautiful baby girl.

11

WELCOME TO THE 80s!

THE Hard Rock was still rocking and I couldn't wait to pull on my apron every day. When the 80s arrived, London was a very different place to what it had been in 1971 – and I like to think that in our own way we played a part in helping to lift the city. At the end of the 70s the country had been crippled by strikes and there was a lot of hardship, but the economic bad times didn't seem to affect the Hard Rock and we stayed busy. As our tenth anniversary approached in 1981, the city had learned to chill out and there was a real feeling that there were good times ahead. The minute you went into work you didn't stop. When you went onto that floor with your uniform on at 12 o'clock you just kept going all day.

In 1979, Margaret Thatcher was elected Prime Minister and it was good to see a woman in power for the first time. It was a big change and I think it benefitted the country enormously. A lot of people, especially Americans, were in awe that we had a Prime Minister who was a lady. It was the first and only time it had ever happened. She was a very powerful leader and there was a feeling that Britain was back on the map.

At the Hard Rock we were still doing the thing that we do best – having a good time and working with a smile. One of the things that I remember the most about the 80s are the great parties that we used to throw for all the tennis stars that would flock to London every year for Wimbledon. We used to call it the 'Wimbledon Jam' and all the big names would hang out at the Hard Rock. Arthur Ashe had been the first player to come to us back in the 70s, but the 80s brought a host of new young stars like Pat Cash and Vitas Gerulaitis, who became very good friends with Prab. My favorite was John McEnroe who was as wild as they come (and I mean that as a compliment!). He had a reputation for being rude to tennis umpires and he became famous for arguing with them.

"You cannot be SERIOUS!!!!" he would scream at them, whenever they made a decision he didn't like.

I was working in the restaurant one day when McEnroe joined a group of people at one of my tables. He dragged a spare chair from somewhere and shoved it on the end of a table for four, where the others were already sitting. The next minute he was looking around for a waitress and he waved his arm impatiently and clicked his fingers. I thought he was being a bit cheeky, but I got the impression he had a good sense of humor so I went over and put my arm around his back.

"You are not on the tennis court now, this is my table you know!" I told him.

He laughed and I held up my hand as if to say 'don't call me like that!'

"Anyway, what are you having today?" I continued.

McEnroe ordered a beer and from that point on we always got along together very well. I used to serve him a lot whenever he was in London. He was dating the actress Tatum O'Neal, whom he later married. They were young and funky and I always took time to say hello to them. I loved to watch John play tennis on the television and it was always a thrill to greet him. He played up to his image of being a bit of a wild character and when he walked into the room you got the impression hat he loved all the attention, especially at the parties that we hosted. He was a star and he captivated the room.

Peter Morton loved tennis and all his family would come over during Wimbledon. Isaac was more into hanging out with the rock stars, but for Peter one of the highlights was mixing with all the greats of the tennis world. I once served Peter and his father and grandfather all at the same table while they enjoyed the fun. The tennis crowd loved Prab, who did a very good job at keeping them happy. We used to do a special T-shirt for Wimbledon every year. When McEnroe won the tournament for the third time in 1984, he later wore one of our Hard Rock T-shirts in front of the cameras, which gave a huge boost to our merchandise sales.

The newspapers would go crazy when McEnroe and Pat Cash were in town together, because they were always good for a headline. There was a famous occasion when they grabbed a guitar and were pictured jamming together in the restaurant. I don't know if the guitar they used was given to them or whether they simply ripped it off the wall, which was something they were quite capable of doing if they were in the mood for a party.

Whenever I see John today he always greets me like an old friend. He was in his early 20s when I first met him and it is wonderful to see how he's matured into a gentleman. I bumped into him again a few years ago while I was with Calum MacPherson (our senior VP of Cafe Operations in North America).

"Jeeez, how far do we go back?" I asked McEnroe.

John looked at us with a twinkle in is eye.

"I've known Rita so long, she used to change my diaper!" he said.

* * * * *

EVERYTHING was going great at work but away from the Hard Rock I experienced some difficult times at home. My marriage to Tony started to become shaky and things came to a head in early 1981 when I briefly considered moving back to Ireland.

Peter and Isaac were getting ready to celebrate the tenth anniversary of our opening with a big party and a special pin badge, but all the preparations for the summer passed me by and I don't remember much about them. My problem was that Tony was spending all the time out drinking with the men in his family and it seemed as if we hardly spent any time together. In the mornings I would be the one who got the children ready for school and took them there. I'd rush home and cook a meal before going to the Hard Rock, in order that there would be something to warm up for the family that night. When I got back in the evening Tony was never at home. When he came in at the end of the evening he would be drunk. He was never rude or violent, but he would open a bottle of whiskey or a can of beer and continue drinking so I would just go to bed. The marriage was failing: there was very little affection.

Despite our difficulties, I wanted to make a go of things with Tony. He was a good man at heart – it was just his flaming drinking that used to upset me! Financially, we were doing okay and we'd managed to get mortgages to buy two houses

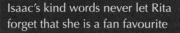

Isaac's kind words never let Rita forget that she is a fan favourite

Rita Rules HRC
SAVE THE PLANET

Hard Rock CAFE

LONDON

ALL IS ONE

MEMORABILIA

GUIDE

TO THE

HALL OF FAME

To Rita
The Heart & Soul
of HRC.

ESTABLISHED JUNE 14TH 1971

150 OLD PARK LANE
LONDON W1

I Love You
FOREVER

LOVE ALL SERVE ALL

ISAAC 3?

Rita, a star in the making, winning the Miss Galway competition

Rita cooking up some memories with a few Hard Rock chefs

Rita with Eve Patrick, Dan Aykroyd, and Isaac Tigrett

Rita's the real rock star as she accepts her honorary MBE from Culture Secretary, Chris Smith, recognizing her services to tourism in Britain, 1998

A beautiful bride, Rita and her husband Tony on their wedding day, June 25th 1964

Rita rubbing shoulders with supermodel Elle Macpherson at Live 8 in Hyde Park, July 2004

Rita shares a sweet moment with the girls and an officer

Getting groovy with the Blue Man Group at the Hard Rock Cafe, Boston, Faneuil Hall, 2007

Rita dancing with Ronnie Wood at the Hard Rock Cafe, London

Striking a pose with Bob Geldof

British icons Rita and Sir Paul McCartney sharing a moment backstage at the Hard Rock Calling Festival, London, 2009

The Hard Rock Calling Festival gets two thumbs up from Rita! Hyde Park, 2011

Rita with Tony Blair backstage at the Brit Awards, February 1996

Rita striking a pose with Mötley Crüe at the grand re-opening of Hard Rock Cafe, New York, 2005

Snoop Dogg showing Rita some love at Live 8 London, Hyde Park, 2005

With her name in lights, Rita celebrates her 50th birthday with Curiosity Killed the Cat, Piccadilly Circus, 1990

Rita sharing a family moment with her mum Cecilia and sister Martina

Rita and Joss Stone happily showing their support for *Imagine There's No Hunger*, Hard Rock Cafe, London, 2008

Rita and Elton John celebrating $150,000 raised for The Elton John AIDS Foundation at the grand opening of Hard Rock Live, Orlando, 1999

When Rita's involved it's always a party! Celebrating with the Hard Rock Cafe London team, 1991

Wow! Rita aged 16, London, 1957

In honour of Fleet Week and Hard Rock's 40th anniversary, Rita recreates the iconic sailor kiss outside the Hard Rock Cafe, Times Square, 2011

Sweet enough to eat! Rita with a cake version of herself at an after party, Hard Rock Cafe, London

Rita sharing a hug with Prab Nallamilli at the grand opening of Hard Rock Cafe, Dallas, 1986

Rita attending the grand opening of Hard Rock Cafe, New York, with her pal Steven Van Zandt and his wife Maureen

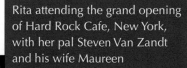

Rita got the best seat in the house after throwing out the first pitch to celebrate Hard Rock's 40th anniversary, Wrigley Field, Chicago, 2011

News of Rita's MBE makes the paper, 1998

They also serve who only rock and wait

A WAITRESS who has served many of the world's leading celebrities is to be appointed an honorary MBE for her services to Britain's tourist industry.

Rita Gilligan, from Co Galway, has worked at the Hard Rock Café in London since it opened in June 1971. Her customers have included Paul Newman, Muhammad Ali, members of the Beatles and the Spice Girls. While still waitressing in London three days a week, she now also travels to new venues as the company's "cultural attaché".

Chris Smith, the Culture Secretary, said: "Rita has given outstanding service to our tourism industry through her work at the Hard Rock Café and is renowned for combining efficient service and a lively approach. Over the years she has been deluged with letters of thanks."

Ms Gilligan said: "I never expected an award. I have always tried to make everyone enjoy their visit, whether they are a star or not, whether they order a T-bone steak or a cup of tea."

Rita Gilligan is both waitress and "cultural attaché" for the Hard Rock Café

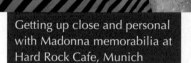

Getting up close and personal with Madonna memorabilia at Hard Rock Cafe, Munich

Rita doing what she does best – serving guests with a smile at Hard Rock Cafe, London, 1971

Not even rain can keep Rita down as she smashes a guitar at Hard Rock Cafe, Prague

Amy MacDonald and Rita smashing hits on the red carpet at the grand re-opening of Hard Rock Cafe, Berlin, 2010

Rita throwing out the first pitch at a Cubs game to celebrate Hard Rock's 40th anniversary, Wrigley Field, Chicago, 2011

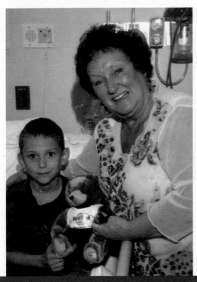

Hard Rock International CEO Hamish Dodds and Rita celebrating 40 years at Hard Rock Calling Festival, London, 2011

Rita sharing a smile and a teddy bear with Little Joey at the Joe DiMaggio Children's Hospital, Miami

Rita and Bruce Springsteen, all smiles backstage at Hard Rock Calling Festival, Hyde Park, London, 2009

Hard Rock Calling, 2011

Elizabeth R

Elizabeth the Second, *by the Grace of God of the United Kingdom of Great Britain and Northern Ireland and of Her other Realms and Territories Queen, Head of the Commonwealth, Defender of the Faith and Sovereign of the Most Excellent Order of the British Empire to Mrs. Rita Gilligan*

Greeting

Whereas *We have thought fit to nominate and appoint you to be an Honorary Member of the Civil Division of Our said Most Excellent Order of the British Empire*

We do *by these presents grant unto you the Dignity of an Honorary Member of Our said Order and hereby authorise you to have hold and enjoy the said Dignity and Rank of an Honorary Member of Our aforesaid Order together with all and singular the privileges thereunto belonging or appertaining.*

Given *at Our Court at Saint James's under Our Sign Manual and the Seal of Our said Order this Tenth day of February 1998 in the Forty-seventh year of Our Reign.*

By the Sovereign's Command.

Rita's honorary MBE letter from
Queen Elizabeth II and Prince Philip

Rita and the London team posing with a giant cake to celebrate 20 years of the Hard Rock Cafe, 1991

Rita with her grandson Ryan, celebrating 44 years at the Hard Rock Cafe, London

Rita's 20-month old grandson Howard rockin' it out!

in Ireland. Tony worked in the property industry so he knew how to negotiate with the banks so getting the loans had been no problem.

I loved working at the Hard Rock but it seemed to me that Tony was never going to change his ways while we were in London. I thought that perhaps if we went back to Ireland together things would be better. I had an idea that we would be able to lead a life that was more like a normal married couple there, spending time together and going to church on Sundays. I was confused because I didn't want to leave the Hard Rock, but I knew we couldn't go on the way we were. In the end, I decided to ask for some time off work so that Tony and I could spend some time in Ireland while we tried to work things out. While we were there we could make arrangements to rent out one of the houses, which would bring in a little extra money to help with the mortgages. I would decide what to do about work after that. When Peter and Isaac found out they did their best to persuade me to stay in England. They were worried that if I went to Ireland I wouldn't come back, which was a possibility. Peter was playing pinball at the machine near the bar when he called me over to discuss it one afternoon.

"Miss Rita, I hear you are thinking of going to Ireland. Why is that?" he asked.

I was a bit embarrassed to speak about my marriage so I glossed over it and just said that Tony and I were having a few problems.

"We have mortgages on two houses and we need to arrange to rent one of them out," I added.

Peter looked me in the eye and I could see that I had his full attention.

"Rita, if you stay I will pay your mortgages," he said.

I was speechless. It was a wonderful gesture and it confirmed what I'd always known – that despite his frosty exterior, underneath it all Peter was a kind and generous man. But there was no way I could possibly accept his offer.

"That's very kind Peter," I said. "But I have to say no, because I want to give this a try myself. I want to make a go of things."

On my last day before going to Ireland I felt very sad, although I was relieved that I might finally be able to work it out with Tony. Isaac was in the restaurant that afternoon and when things slowed down after the lunchtime rush he called me over. He was stood next to Vera, our cashier at the time.

"How much money is in the cash till?" he asked.

Vera went and counted and it came to just over £900. Isaac must have sent somebody to the bank to top it up because later that day he called me over again and wished me luck. He then handed me an envelope.

Inside there was £1000 in cash.

It was more money that I had ever held in my life and it brought tears to my eyes. It felt like I'd been through thick and thin with Isaac and Peter over the last ten years. They agreed I could take time off with a view to going back if that's what I decided to do. The money was their way of telling me that I was part of the family and that they wanted to help me. They could sense I was struggling and worried about the mortgages. I thanked Isaac for his kindness and I went straight to the bank and used the money to pay off some of what we owed.

* * * * *

THINGS got worse between Tony and I in Ireland. His drinking became constant and in a small community like Galway people soon began to talk. The plan was to find some work while we were deciding what to do but Tony refused to do anything that he felt was beneath him. The problem was that there was no work as a surveyor in Galway, so he slipped into a pattern of drinking during the day. He'd end up in the bars down by the docks in the early hours and his drinking became heavier and heavier. Things were still very old-fashioned in Galway and it was frowned upon for a woman to be the breadwinner while her husband refused to work. I think my parents could see that it was slowly killing me and one day my dad asked to speak to me. We were alone together on a green overlooking the bay.

"Rita, your mother and I are ashamed because he is out drinking while you are working," he said to me. "You are better off going back to England with the children."

Then he handed me a small envelope.

"There you are girl, this is for you – but don't tell Tony," he added.

Inside the envelope there was £200. I went home and gave half of it to Tony, but I knew my father was right about going back to England. I told Tony that I was going back to London for a couple of weeks to think about things. I'd been back two days when my friend Betty told me that Isaac had asked her to pass on a message to me.

"He's heard that you're back and he wants you to go and see him at the Hard Rock," she explained.

When I walked into the restaurant I felt a mixture of warmth and relief, it felt like I'd come home. When I saw Isaac he gave me a great big smile and we sat at the big circular table in the middle of the restaurant. He took my hands and put them on the table and reached out and put his own hands on top of mine.

"Miss Rita, come back to us," he said.

I promised him I'd think about it and afterwards I spent a bit of time on the restaurant floor with the girls. Tony's mother was looking after Tara for me while I was in London and later that night I told her how happy I'd felt back in the Hard Rock.

"Why don't you go in and do a couple of days work there while you're here?" she suggested.

I thought about what she said and I agreed I'd do a couple of shifts while I was in town, even if it was just to see my customers, as we had quite a few regulars whom I regarded as friends. When I went in and put my apron on again I had a wonderful feeling. The fun came back into my life and the two days flew by. I knew then that the Hard Rock was going to be the path that I chose, not Ireland.

I went back to Galway briefly to see Tony. Tara had her Holy Communion coming up there and we wanted it to be a family occasion in Ireland – but after that I was determined to return to London for good. I sat down with Tony and I explained my decision.

"Tony I think we should go back to London," I said.

"Rita, I think I will stay here and things will be alright," he replied.

Tony had found a lifestyle that he liked in Ireland. He would sometimes go down to the beach with a big easel and paint on a canvas during the day, while he enjoyed a drink. He loved the countryside and the wildlife and he also liked to go fishing.

"I am going to go back to London," I told him.

Tony was very laid back about it and said it would be okay. He was going to stay in Ireland. He never worried about anything, except perhaps where the next pint was coming from. I was sad that we'd be apart, but at the same time I was excited about carrying on with my job working for Isaac and Peter.

When I returned to the Hard Rock it felt like I was in Heaven. All the pressure of trying to make the marriage work lifted from me. I felt like I was my old self again and I was surrounded by friends. I realized that I had lost myself for a couple of months because I had so much on my mind, but now I'd found myself.

I was Rita again.

12

A ROCK 'N' ROLL DIVORCE: PETER AND ISAAC SPLIT

THE days that followed after I resumed my role at the Hard Rock were among some of the happiest times of my life. Not only was I free to get on with the job that I loved but London now had a real buzz about it. With Maggie Thatcher in Downing Street during the 80s it felt like there was a great boom on the way, although not everybody was a fan of hers. Many people didn't like her way of doing things but I'm in favor of powerful women – and I admired the fact that she didn't take any crap!

Working in the heart of London meant that I often got to see world events close at hand. The country was given a huge boost by the royal wedding when Prince Charles married Lady Diana at St Paul's Cathedral. It seemed as if the whole nation was in love with Diana and at the Hard Rock we were no different. Years later when we were celebrating our 15th anniversary, Isaac has some bomber jackets made with the Hard Rock logo on the back. We decided to send a few round to Buckingham Palace – after all the Royal Family were our neighbors! The first three were made for The Queen, Prince Philip and The Queen Mother. Isaac also arranged to send one to Princess Diana. They were cheeky gifts because the Queen was hardly likely to go out on the balcony of the palace wearing a bomber jacket!

We got a letter back from the Palace to thank us for the gesture, but they explained that they were returning the jackets because they wouldn't be wearing them. But Princess Diana must have had other ideas because we were later amazed when she visited a theme park wearing our prized jacket. She was the coolest fashion icon on the planet so the photographs went all around the world. Just like John McEnroe's T-shirt, it helped the Hard Rock to become a recognized name all over the planet!

On the day of Diana's wedding to Prince Charles it was very busy in the restaurant. London was packed with tourists and well wishers and because the restaurant is next to Green Park we were right at the heart of the celebrations. The security in town that day was very tight because there had been a lot of problems with the IRA, who'd launched a number of bomb attacks in the UK. It wasn't unusual for restaurants to receive bomb threats by telephone in those days. We had a few scares but thankfully they were hoax calls. We had a special code name that would be announced over the loudspeakers so that the staff knew when to evacuate all the customers, as you can't be too careful. We'd comp all their bills and ask them leave before getting ourselves out while the police checked the building. On one occasion, Isaac took us all over to the InterContinental Hotel nearby. We were all still in our uniforms but he led us into the bar and we had a bit of a party while we waited for the police to give us the all clear!

On the day of the Royal wedding the security services were up on our roof to keep an eye on things in the park and when I went into our bar area there were four great big guys there who were dressed in dark suits and they were having a quiet drink. We knew they were connected to Diana in some way and I presumed that they were members of the SAS, who were on call in case there was any trouble. In fact, the day passed off like a dream. The weather was wonderful and the whole city was a sea of happy crowds waving flags and cheering the Royals. We had the wedding event playing on the TV all day in the restaurant and there were lots of Americans there who all loved her. I'd been working on the night that the Royal engagement was announced and I can still remember Dian's smile as she paraded in front of the cameras in a blue outfit with the world's biggest sparkler on her finger!

I never actually saw Diana in the Hard Rock but Prince Andrew visited us a couple of times with Koo Stark, the American actress whom he was dating at the time. She was very beautiful and I saw them together at a private a party that we hosted. I always thought they'd get wed but it wasn't to be. Many years later, after Prince Andrew married Sarah Ferguson (or Fergie as we call her), I served their daughters Princess Beatrice and Princess Eugenie when they came to a children's birthday party at the Hard Rock. They were aged about four and five at the time and they were having a wild time rushing around the restaurant with their friends. I was worried that they'd try to go upstairs to the roof so I asked the Royal bodyguards to keep an eye on them! When I called the children back to their table because their food was ready, Princess Beatrice was so excited that as she sat down she slipped and banged her chin on the table. Luckily, she was fine and she gave me a little smile afterwards.

"You see...that's what you get for rushing!" I said.

* * * * *

ISAAC and Peter were a great double act – but after more than ten years together they finally decided to go their separate ways, which came as a huge shock to everybody at the Hard Rock. During their time in business they'd turned a crazy idea for a rock cafe into one of the most famous restaurants on the planet. It was a great achievement, but as time went on I noticed the relationship between them had become more distant. There was still a connection between them but I got the impression that they didn't mix very much away from work. Having said that, if one of them was drowning I think the other would have jumped in to save him – but they were very different in their outlook. Peter was very quiet whereas Isaac could also be very loud when he was excited. He'd shout across the bar to Peter to come and join him but you rarely saw them sitting together and sharing a drink.

Isaac and Peter had been very kind to me and I felt huge loyalty to them both. Other people saw our success at the Hard Rock and they were keen to try and copy us. The bosses of other restaurants, who wanted to lure me away from the Hard Rock, would occasionally approach me but I always turned them down. There one gentleman who offered to give me my own apartment in a posh part of London if I agreed to move. His name was Bob Payton and he was an American businessman who would drop by the Hard Rock and sit at our counter. He seemed fascinated by everything we did.

"Rita, where do you get your tomatoes?" he'd asked.

I soon realized that he was asking questions because he wanted to open a string of restaurants of his own. He had a huge apartment in Tottenham Court Road, which he offered to give me if I jumped ship.

"Rita, if you join me it's all yours," he said.

I was flattered but I said no thank you. I loved the Hard Rock too much. Isaac and Peter had shown me so much kindness that I could never consider leaving them (Bob went on to achieve huge success with the restaurant chain The Chicago Pizza Pie Factory which first opened in London, but he was later tragically killed in a car crash after selling up for millions).

It was in the spring of 1982 that the staff started to hear rumors that Peter and Isaac were about to go their separate ways. I hated the idea of them parting company because for me it felt like there was about to be a split in the family. I decided to ask Prab what was happening.

"Is Peter leaving us?" I asked him outright.

Prab was a genius who had helped to build up the restaurant so he was hugely respected by both Peter and Isaac. He wasn't able to say anything at the time because he was very professional, but things came to a head the next morning. One of the staff had heard something on the radio about a management change at the Hard Rock. It shows how far we'd come that something like that was big news. The staff were all buzzing with the gossip but nobody seemed to know what was going on. Then Isaac arrived at the restaurant and he called everybody together. We gathered in a circle at the front of the restaurant before we opened for the day and Isaac stood in the doorway with Maureen Starkey at his side. He was wearing a black suit that looked like it as made of silk. The expression on his face was very serious.

"Guys, there is going to be a change, " he told us.

The exact words that he used next are a bit of a blur to me because I was shocked, but he basically told us that Peter would be leaving London and that somebody new would be coming into the company. Isaac didn't speak for very long and he left us soon afterwards. I don't know for sure but I think that he may have been upset. There was no sign of Peter.

We spent the rest of the day in limbo: it seemed as if my worst fears had been confirmed and that the Hard Rock family was splitting up. In fact, Isaac and Peter had done a deal whereby they divided up their separate plans for America. The details were complicated but in simple terms it meant that Peter would retain the rights to use the Hard Rock name anywhere west of the Mississippi river, with Isaac retaining everything to the east (with the exception of Chicago, which Peter would take, and Dallas, which Isaac would take). Meanwhile Isaac would continue to own Hard Rock Cafe in London, so it basically meant that I would be saying goodbye to Peter, who would now be based on the other side of the world. I would miss him and his moody ways. He could be a grumpy bastard at times, but I loved him (Peter, if you're reading this today, I still adore you)!

We didn't hear much more until two weeks later when the staff were called to a meeting at the end of the afternoon. I was getting ready to go home to my kids after a busy shift but we were all asked to attend. Peter came in, wearing jeans and a smart black jacket. He was accompanied by an Englishman in a formal suit with a big kipper tie (I thought he looked a bit like Al Capone!).

"This is Barry Cox and he will be replacing me," Peter told us.

Peter was relaxed and calm and it was clear to me that this was his farewell speech. Afterwards we were all invited over to the Rose & Crown pub opposite the restaurant. I went to join them and was delighted to see Isaac and Peter sitting together at table sharing a beer. The tension that sometimes existed when they were together seemed to have vanished and some of the old warmth that they felt for each other seemed to have returned.

When I asked them about their plans Isaac looked at me with a smile and said: "Miss Rita – it is like a divorce."

Isaac was spot on because that's exactly what it felt like. A rock and roll divorce, albeit an amicable one.

Later that evening I got chatting to Barry Cox and I discovered that he was a wonderful man. He'd had a small role as character in the movie *The Italian Job* and he was very well connected. I thought he'd fit in well at the Hard Rock, although I wondered what the customers would make of his formal business suit.

"Barry, the management here normally wear jeans," I whispered to him.

The next day Barry came to work in an open-necked shirt!

* * * * *

THERE was a shock in store for me later that year, but this time it was caused by events outside of the Hard Rock. It happened on a beautiful summer day in July and it's one of the saddest memories that I have.

I was getting off the bus outside The Hilton on my way to work when I heard a deep, rumbling bang. It was a horrible noise, like thunder, only more sinister. It was coming from the direction of Hyde Park, which I knew would be packed with tourists. For a few moments afterwards there was an uneasy silence and the air seemed to be very still. Then as I walked on down the road I began to hear wailing ambulances and police sirens. Not just one, but it sounded like dozens of them.

It was a bomb attack.

This time it was no hoax and when I arrived at the Hard Rock I discovered the terrible news. The IRA had launched simultaneous terror attacks in both Regents Park and Hyde Park, which was right on our doorstep. We had a television switched on in the restaurant and we watched as the full horror of the events unfolded. It was a strange feeling, viewing it on the screen knowing that it was all happening just a few hundred yards away.

Four soldiers from the Royal Horse Guards had been killed in Hyde Park and seven bandsmen from the Royal Green Jackets had lost their lives in Regent's Park. Those terrible images from the TV set will be burned into my memory for the rest of my life. Seven horses were killed in one of the explosions and their bodies were a pitiful sight, as they lay lifeless in the road. Tourists from all over the world came to London to see the soldiers and their beautiful animals. I hated that fact that the carnage had been caused by problems back in my native Ireland and it upset me a great deal.

We opened very late that day but nobody was very interested in eating. In the end, we just put out a few bowls of crisps and we gave out free drinks to the odd tourist who came in for a rest. We explained that the kitchens would probably stay closed for the rest of the afternoon.

It was a very dark day.

13

THE BIG APPLE: HARD ROCK CAFE SPREADS ITS WINGS!

WHEN Isaac and Peter went their separate ways it was an important moment because it showed the Hard Rock was ready to spread its wings around the world. We'd come a long way and we'd done it by sticking to our irresistible recipe of great service and food topped off with rock 'n' roll music. Even though we'd said farewell to Peter in London, we still had a wonderful family spirit. Barry Cox brought a fresh energy while his connections and expertise helped to keep the customers flowing in. Prab was also now very much at the forefront of everything and he and Isaac formed a very close bond.

"Our ethos was don't worry about making money – just take care of one another," recalls Prab today. "There was a fantastic pioneering spirit about the place."

Prab is convinced that one of the reasons that we had the edge over our competitors at the time was because our staff all worked together as one team. In most other businesses at the time the front of house staff (like the waiters and waitresses) were run as a separate group from what was known as the 'back of house', which included the chefs and the rest of the kitchen and cleaning staff. But at the Hard Rock we all cooperated very closely which meant that we could communicate together and quickly give the customers whatever they wanted. If I was serving a businessman who was in a rush for his lunch I'd ask the chef to get his skates on. We could turn around orders at great speed for diners who wanted a quick meal before going on their way. Our staff were the lifeblood of the company and we realized that good teamwork was the answer to everything. It was the perfect approach and we were voted as the best restaurant in London in several polls, ahead of great places like Langan's Brasserie (where Princess Diana famously used to dine!).

Of course, as well as looking after one another we also made money for the company, lots of it. But as I said earlier we always tried to give a little back. Isaac continued to be very interested in charitable work and the spiritual side of life was very important to him. Sometimes he would clasp his hands in from of him as if he were praying while he explained his vision to me.

"Miss Rita – I would like to give ten per cent of the takings to God," he said.

Isaac was as good as his word and he got involved in some wonderful projects around the world to help the needy. Our policy of helping others is still a big part of Hard Rock culture today. I'm very privileged to still be able to do a lot of work with great causes like Nordoff Robbins (a musical therapy charity dedicated to transforming the lives of vulnerable children and adults) and The Chickenshed Theatre (a theatrical charity that works with schools and which has been providing support for people with challenging medical conditions since 1974).

With London being such a huge success it seemed only natural that we would expand to other great cities. Peter went to

Los Angeles where he opened a Hard Rock Cafe in 1982 along similar lines to London and it wasn't long before Isaac and Prab developed expansion plans of their own. I was walking up the stairs from the basement one morning in January to start my shift when Isaac broke the news to me. Prab was at his side and Isaac had a big smile on his face.

"Miss Rita – I am taking you to America! You are going to train our staff in New York," he said.

I was shocked because I'd seen very little of the world apart from London and Galway.

"My God! Can it really be true that I am going to America," I thought.

Isaac rushed off elsewhere without saying much more but later Prab explained what they had in mind. We were going to open a huge new restaurant on 57th Street in Manhattan, right at the heart of the Big Apple. The scale of their plans was enormous. In London we'd started off with about 46 staff, but in New York there would need to be around 150 to 200. The restaurant was to be split across two levels with a grand staircase and a huge mezzanine. There were two dining areas and two separate bars, one of which would be shaped like a giant guitar. The centerpiece was to be a giant 'God Wall' that would greet customers as they walked in. The wall was Isaac's own idea and it would be decorated with symbols that represented all the great religions and cultural icons of the world. It was to be the perfect embodiment of *Love All…All is One.* I had no idea about what it would all cost but it was obvious that it would require millions of dollars of investment and it showed how confident we had now become. We were ready to serve the world!

"We want you to play an important part in everything by going to New York in order to tell all the new staff how we do things in London," Prab explained.

I was to be accompanied by one of our other seasoned waitresses, Eve, who was a colorful character. I suspected that together we'd have a ball, it all sounded amazing and I had to pinch myself to believe it was really happening. The new restaurant was to be decorated with an amazing array of rock 'n' roll memorabilia, which is something that Isaac had been planning for some time while he'd been looking for a location in New York. Prab later told me that Isaac had become friendly with a contact in the rock industry called Brian Murphy, who had an enormous collection of rock memorabilia that he kept in three big warehouses in New Jersey. We already had the start of a great collection of our own in London, but Isaac wanted to take things to the next level in New York. With Brian's help, Isaac got his hands on some fabulous treasures and he later asked a member of staff called Steve Routhier to help catalog everything that we owned. Steve was a true Hard Rocker with a great personality and he became the curator of our early collection, which has grown to an enormous size today.

Isaac had also lined up some powerful investors for the New York restaurant. They included a well-known banker from Tennessee called Jock Weaver III. Yul Brynner was also on board and his son Rock would be joining us there too. Meanwhile, the actor Dan Aykroyd agreed to be our Director of Public Awareness to help spread the word. Dan was the hottest name in Hollywood at the time having starred in *The Blues Brothers* and *Ghostbusters* (which was due to be released later that year). It was an amazing plan and I couldn't wait to see it in all action!

* * * * *

IT was the first time I'd been on a jumbo jet and when and I boarded it looked to me as if the rows of seats in the passenger cabin seemed to go on forever.

"Jeez – is this a plane or what? It feels like we are walking to America!" I joked as we made our way along the aisle.

Eve was very intelligent English woman, aged about 15 years older than me, who had been at the Hard Rock in London since the beginning, just like I had. She had originally worked as an actress and liked to have a good drink. In London, she'd always be sipping a glass of wine and she was good company. When we arrived at JFK airport in New York it felt like I was walking into another world. I was shocked by the scale and noise of it all. There seemed to be policemen all over the place and everywhere we looked there were hundreds of yellow cabs picking up passengers. Unfortunately there was nobody there to meet us and we weren't sure where to go, so we decided to call Isaac.

"We're here at the airport – but we're stuck," we explained after we eventually managed to get through on the phone.

"Don't worry ladies, I'm sending a car," he replied.

After a bit of a wait we were taken to a Holiday Inn that was located close to where the Hard Rock was going to be on 57th Street. One thing that we noticed straight away in America was that everybody expected a tip, no matter what! When our car pulled up at the Holiday Inn, somebody opened the door for us and as I got out a man had his hand held out. He wanted money. When we were inside the hotel somebody else carried our bags for what seemed like five yards – and out came the hand again. Eve and I realized why our American customers in London were such good tippers – it was drummed into them! We duly handed over a few dollars after we were shown to our rooms, which were very comfortable. Isaac's father John had business connections with The Holiday Inn so I guess he knew that it was a good place for us to stay. It seemed like we had been travelling for an eternity and I was grateful to crash into bed.

The next morning I got up early and decided to go for a walk because I was keen to see a bit of New York before going to the Hard Rock. Eve was nowhere to be seen, so I assumed she was having a rest because she sometimes liked to enjoy a late tipple. When I got outside the sites of the city nearly took my breath away. The yellow cabs were still everywhere but it was the huge buildings that stunned me the most. I walked along craning my neck to look up at all the skyscrapers that seemed to stretch right up into the clouds. I was fascinated. When I needed to cross the road I assumed it was okay to just walk across at a convenient moment when there was a gap in the traffic. But when I got to the middle all the cars started to honk their horns in anger.

Beep. Beep. Beep.

"Jeez, they're all flaming mad here!" I thought, as I dodged across the street.

I'd only been in America for half a day and I was beginning to wonder what I'd let myself in for. But I needn't have worried because the New Yorkers turned out to be wonderful people. They are real characters and they wear their hearts on sleeves –

they're friendly but they're not afraid to show a bit of spirit and attitude when it matters. I battled on with crossing through the traffic and then I saw the outside of the Hard Rock in New York for first time.

It was amazing.

It was enormous and the restaurant took up what seemed to be the front of a grand building that dominated the street. There was a big sign on it that said Hard Rock Cafe and above it high on the wall, was the rear end of a Cadillac with its wheels and tailfin hanging out into thin air. It was the back end of an old 50s model and the car had been suspended there to make it look like it had crashed into the building! It was just one of the crazy ideas that Isaac and his advisors had dreamed up to catch people's attention – and boy did it do the trick.

The interior of the restaurant was awesome and my jaw dropped when I when I saw it for the first time. There was soft lighting that made it feel dark and comfortable inside compared with the harsh daylight on the street. I could see straight away that the place was huge! Isaac had knocked two levels into one into in order to create an amazing amount of height and space for the mezzanine area. The grand staircase looked as if it could easily have been at home in Buckingham Palace. There were little statutes mounted alongside it so that as you walked up the staircase you passed a mini Statue of Liberty and other iconic symbols. When you got to the top, the view from the balcony across the mezzanine was spectacular. I loved to stand there and watch people coming in and out of the restaurant down below. Close to the entrance on the ground floor there was a sumptuous bar shaped like an enormous Fender guitar.

This was rock 'n' roll through and through.

On the upper level there was another bar called 'The Poor Boy's 21 Club'. The name was a reference to New York's famous 21 Club, where the Big Apple's elite and wealthy went to socialize together. The message was clear: the Hard Rock was just as grand – but you didn't need to be rich to be treated like a millionaire here!

The most spectacular feature of all was Isaac's God Wall, which dominated the view as diners looked up from their tables. It was decorated with symbolic images each of which represented a different cultural icon. There was a Virgin Mary and Jesus to represent Christianity, a Star of David to represent the Jewish faith; and in the middle underneath a big horseshoe was Isaac's own spiritual guru, Sai Baba. Inside the horseshoe was a message that said: 'Who do you love?' There was also a big picture of Elvis Presley for rock 'n' roll fans, an image of pills to represent drugs and a gold krugerrand, which I guessed was there for anybody who worshipped money. Across the top of the wall, in giant capitals was another sign that said:

'ALL IS ONE'

The message was simple: it doesn't matter who you are or what you believe, everybody is welcome at the Hard Rock. One or two people on the staff were concerned that some customers might get the wrong idea and think that it was disrespectful to show religious icons in a rock 'n' roll setting, but they needn't have worried – the public understood the message perfectly. When Isaac greeted me in the restaurant I could see the excitement glimmering in his bright blue eyes.

"Miss Rita – what do you think?" he asked, as he gazed around the new restaurant.

"Isaac – I think it's going to be great!" I said.

Unfortunately, what we didn't know was there were plenty of hiccups that lay ahead.

* * * * *

LOTS of the waiters and waitresses that we hired were out of work actors or aspiring writers and there were some wonderful personalities among them. Many of them already had a lot of great experience working in restaurants and hotels – but Eve and I were there to teach them how to do things the Hard Rock way.

"Listen guys – this is not like working at The Russian Tea Room or The Wolseley…you're a Hard Rocker now!" I explained.

Eve and I told them about how we treated customers in London and we explained about double-checking and Southern hospitality.

"Don't be afraid to pull up a chair and talk to the customers," I said. "If there's a group of four lads and there's a spare space then sit down with them and join in with the fun."

We planned to model New York closely on London in many ways; right down to making sure the burgers tasted the same. We flew in our own butcher from London to work with our supplier in New York to make sure that everything was perfect. As the grand opening approached we were full of confidence but I had a few nagging doubts. I was worried about a new computer system that had been devised for taking the orders. In London the waitresses did this in the traditional way with a pen and pad. A copy of the hand-written chit was given to the kitchen in order to process the order. In New York, we were about to switch to a computerized system for the first time. Instead of handing in a chit, every waitress had to go to a computer screen and select each item using a code. Each waitress had her own number (I was 23!) and the computer would record the table number, the number of guests and a number for every item that they ordered. The machine would then automatically generate a chit, which would go to the kitchen. In theory, it sounded great – but I was worried about the time it took to tap in the orders.

"What if the machine goes wrong?" I asked one of the technical team who had been brought in to train us on the new system.

"It won't go wrong, besides if anything unexpected happens then there will be people around who you can ask for help."

I wasn't completely convinced but there were also plenty of other things to worry about. There were still workmen painting railings and adjusting all the fixtures right up until the last minute. Isaac had decided to throw a huge preview party on the Thursday before we opened to the public on the following Monday in mid-March. It was a very proud moment when all the new staff gathered at their stations while we waited for the guests to arrive. All the waiters and waitresses seemed to have perfect white teeth and their brilliant smiles reminded me of diamonds scattered around the restaurant in the soft light. Eve and I didn't join in with the waitressing but we were there to keep an eye on things, which meant that I got to see all the fun! There were some very big stars in attendance and I can remember chatting with the Hollywood actresses Lauren Bacall and Liza Minnelli. Meanwhile, Rock Brynner was giving groups of people tours of the place and pointing out all the memorabilia that was on show. Rock explained that there was still plenty more on its way, including Elvis's white suit from Graceland and a guitar that had belonged to Jimi Hendrix. Dan Aykroyd was also in great form, entertaining guests and talking to the press. He told the New York Times that the Hard Rock Cafe in New York was going to be a 'mini-Smithsonian of Rock and Roll.'* Dan and Isaac put on chef hats to help serve up some of the very first burgers to come out from the kitchen and the a pair of them posed for a publicity photo together with Eve and I. It's one of my favorite photographs from over the years!

I later sat down upstairs with Dan and his family and we had a good chat and I told them that I was from Ireland.

"Have you said hello to Eddie Murphy yet?" Dan Aykroyd asked me a bit later on.

Believe it or not I hadn't heard of Eddie Murphy at the time, even though he was already a big star after appearing in *48 Hours* and *Trading Places* (Beverley Hills Cop was due out later that year). I assumed that because Murphy is an Irish name, Eddie must have been somebody from Ireland.

"Er…no. I haven't met him," I replied.

"Come on – I'll introduce you," said Dan, grabbing me by the hand and leading me to the grand staircase. The room was packed with people enjoying the party and we walked down the stairs together.

"Ed, Ed! Say hello to Rita," Dan called out.

I was expecting to meet a burly Paddy but walking towards me was a slim African-American who looked every inch a polished movie star.

"With a name like Murphy I thought you were going to be an Irishman," I said.

"I'm a black Paddy!" Eddie replied, with a big broad grin.

The party was a huge success and it attracted a huge amount of press attention. The Hard Rock had come to town.

Unfortunately, when we opened to the public four days later the teething problems started. In fact, if I am honest our first two days of trading in New York were a bit of a disaster. The electronic system for taking orders turned out to be a nightmare to get used to. It took a lot longer than expected to key things into the computers, which meant that queues of waitresses sometimes started to build up at the screens located at various points around the restaurant. If the person in front of you had to put in an order for a large table it meant that you'd be forced to wait in line for ages. It took a long time for staff to hook up and get used to the correct code numbers, so everything slowed down to a crawl. The orders just didn't seem to be getting through to the kitchen in good time.

Meanwhile, the chefs were having problems of their own. We discovered that the gas pressure in the building wasn't strong enough for peak periods so the kitchen staff had trouble keeping the grills hot. The food arrived too slowly and it was lukewarm, so as a result lots of customers had their bills comped. One or two of the chefs were also slow to catch on about how to prepare the food.

There was one chef in particular who was being rude to the waitresses and screaming and shouting. Prab, who had an important role to play in everything, tried to calm the chef down but eventually he had to tell him to leave. This meant Prab had to go into the kitchen himself to oversee things, which gained him a huge amount of respect from the other staff. Eve and I did what we could to help but there wasn't a great deal we could do about the computer system.

I went down to the ladies room for a brief rest and sat on a chair there in my uniform. A few moments later a guest came in and as she walked past, she left a coin next to me. I realized that she must have thought I was a rest room attendant and she had left me a tip!

It took a few weeks to sort out the problems with the computers and the gas and we had some very poor reviews for the food. The New York Times' food critic later described our burgers as 'slightly-sinewy' and he went on to say that our salads were bland. It turned out that the Mayor's office also hated the Cadillac sign outside, which they said distracted drivers and eventually it had to be removed.

The strange thing was that none of those negative things seemed to matter to the customers. Despite everything, The New York Times joked that judging from the crowds we were attracting, you'd think our burgers were garnished with $50 bills! We were hip, fun and friendly – and the public loved us. It took us a while to get things right there but the Big Apple and the Hard Rock were made for each other.

New York was just the beginning. In 1986 Prab moved to Dallas to oversee a new restaurant there. It was the start of an expansion program that was to eventually see a Hard Rock open up in virtually every major city on the planet.

We were ready to serve the world!

14

LIVE AID: THE GREATEST SHOW ON EARTH

WATCHING Freddie Mercury throw himself about on stage at Live Aid is one of my greatest memories. He looked fantastic in his white jump suit and I was lucky enough to see it all from just a few yards away as I peeked from backstage. It was the greatest show on earth and I'll never forget it.

By 1985, the Hard Rock was the most famous rock 'n' roll restaurant on the planet and we were very honored to be asked to help with Live Aid. It was a boiling hot summer in London and a young singer called Bob Geldof was making headlines after declaring war on poverty. Sir Bob is a household name today for his charity work – and I've had the pleasure of meeting him and his lovely children on many occasions – but back then he was more famous for being the lead singer of The Boomtown Rats, an Irish rock band that had a number of big hits, including *I Don't Like Mondays*.

Live Aid was organized to raise money for millions of starving people in Africa, who desperately needed help. Bob's fiery energy and amazing character helped to persuade loads of musicians to record a song called *Feed The World*, which had gone to Number 1 in December 1984 and raised a lot of money along the way. The idea came in response to terrible scenes of starvation in Ethiopia, a part of the world that had been blighted by years of drought and famine. People across the globe had been shocked by the images of hungry children on the TV news.

When *Feed the World* was released it got a huge amount of attention. Geldof followed up by vowing to raise millions by organizing a huge concert at Wembley Stadium in London in the summer. When he announced his plans they were very ambitious. The line-up read like a Who's Who of the cream of rock, with dozens of major artists agreeing to take part. In the UK, the stars included Paul McCartney, Elton John, David Bowie, Queen, U2, Dire Straits, The Who and, last but not least, my old friends Status Quo. A crowd of nearly 80,000 in the stadium would watch the show live, with millions more expected to tune in on TV from around the planet.

Meanwhile there was to be a simultaneous live gig on the other side of The Atlantic in Philadelphia where the musicians performing live were to include Madonna, Billy Ocean, Bryan Adams, The Beach Boys and members of The Rolling Stones. In fact, there were so many big names that it's almost impossible to mention them all! They were all giving their services for free and every penny raised would go to Africa.

Geldof teamed up with the famous music promoter Harvey Goldsmith, who had strong links to the Hard Rock. Isaac immediately offered to help by volunteering to do all the hospitality at the event for free. When he told us about the plans I was gob-smacked.

"Guys, we are going to recreate the Hard Rock at Wembley," he told us.

Isaac explained that we were going to set up a full-size version of our London restaurant at the event. We would be responsible for feeding all of the stars along with all the VIPs who were due to attend. We'd all shed a tear while we watched those terrible images on TV of starving children in Africa and we were keen to help in any way that we could. The whole staff agreed to give up our time for free – we wanted to put in 100 per cent effort.

It was the first time the Hard Rock had organized hospitality at such a major outside event and it turned out to be a mammoth task. Wembley Stadium is nearly ten miles to the north of where our restaurant is located in Central London. We would be catering for hundreds of people and everything – and I do mean *everything* – had to be transported up to Wembley by our staff in a fleet of vehicles. Today we are experts at hosting outside events like *Hard Rock Calling* and we have access to all the mobile catering equipment that you could possibly need. But back then things were very different. It all happened very quickly and it seemed like we only had a couple of weeks to make it all come to together.

"We're going to need everybody to do their very best," Prab explained. "The restaurant at Old Park Lane will still be open as normal on the day of the concert so it's going to be all hands on deck!"

For two or three days prior to the event we organized a steady convey of cars, vans and trucks that we used to ferry all our gear up to Wembley. We took tables, plates, glasses, bottles, cutlery, burgers and beers... it seemed to go on forever! We also took guitars and other items of memorabilia to decorate the walls in order to make sure that we gave the place the authentic atmosphere of the Hard Rock. We even made sure that we had the same blue and white table covers that we used in the London restaurant. We had a staff of about 120 at the time and nearly half of us went up to Wembley, while the other half worked around the clock to keep things ticking over in Central London. Incredibly, our colleagues at the Hard Rock in the United States were also doing a similar thing for the Live Aid gig in Philadelphia, so Isaac had put us in the fantastic position of being involved on both sides of the Atlantic.

There was huge press interest from around the world and the excitement of being involved was amazing. Sometimes our drivers would lose their way slightly and we'd arrive at the wrong entrance to the stadium and we'd end up having to hump boxes across the parking lot. I can remember carrying a big box of gear up the hill to Wembley, but I didn't mind in the least – I think the adrenalin kept us all going.

* * * * *

WHEN the day of the concert arrived we'd all been working flat out getting everything ready for several days but it didn't prevent everybody from having a big smile on their face. The restaurant was inside a big white marquee tent located behind the stage. It looked beautiful and we were very proud of what we'd created. There was an enormous bar that seemed to run for almost the length of the room and on top of it there were two giant empty glass fishbowls. They were enormous – about a meter wide – and they were put there so that we could collect money in them for charity.

I arrived early at Wembley but the crowds were already starting to gather outside, even though the concert wasn't due to start until later on. We had a pre-shift meeting to run through the plan for the day and the thing I can remember most is that everybody was in such a great mood. We ran though the menu, which contained our Hard Rock & Roll Chili, Bar-B-Que Pork Ribs, plus a selection of sandwiches and burgers. Prab still has an original copy of the menu card at home and on the back there is a huge list of companies and suppliers who had given their services for free. It seemed like everybody in London had pulled together in order to make the event happen in great style.

It was a very hot day with a bright blue sky and as the stadium began to fill up we could hear the crowd cheering and shrieking in excitement. We soon had all the ribs and the burgers ready, but at first it seemed like we had no guests to serve because all the artists were still in their dressing rooms. The idea was that they would come and relax with us after they'd performed on stage, so we had a quiet pause just before the concert got into full swing. My friend Betty was part of the group of staff at Wembley and we chatted for a while.

"Betty – I'm going to have a peek outside onto the stage," I told her.

We weren't supposed to go out front but I couldn't resist going for a sneaky glimpse inside the main stadium.

"Be careful Rita – there will be hell to pay if you get caught," Betty warned me.

The hospitality area was right behind the stage, but it was set back slightly on the one side, so it only took me a few moments to tiptoe my way to the front. I was wearing my white Hard Rock uniform so the security guards and roadies ignored me. When I peeped around the curtain and saw the stadium I was amazed. There was a sea of thousands upon thousands of faces going off into the distance and people were clambering onto each other's shoulders to get a better view. It was a blistering hot day with the sun blazing down and lots of the men were bare-chested. It was so warm that the stage crew had giant hoses and they were spraying water into the crowd in order to keep people cool. What struck me most were all the smiles – everybody seemed to be beaming with joy. I knew then that it was going to be a special day.

I crept back to the hospitality area and told the others what I'd seen. After that we took turns whenever there was a quiet moment to go and have a look up front. The first band on stage was Status Quo. They were greeted by a deafening roar from the crowd before breaking into *Rocking All Over The World*. I knew all the lads in the group quite well by now from bumping into them at the Hard Rock so I was determined to go and watch them perform. Nobody seemed to mind us creeping in and out as long as we kept out of the way. It was amazing to stand there just a few yards away while such an iconic event unfolded. Afterwards the lads were all delighted by the way their set went and they were in the mood to celebrate. They loved to party and they looked happy to see me.

"There she is, there's The Pro!" they joked, using my nickname that they gave me at the Hard Rock. "Rita – we need a drink!"

I brought them a bottle of tequila and I sat chatting with Rick Parfitt and the rest of the lads. They were drinking like fishes and determined to enjoy every moment. David Bowie later came and joined them for a while.

I'd enjoyed watching Status Quo on stage but when it was Freddie Mercury's turn to perform I was blown away. I crept back to my secret place behind the stage and I peeked through at Freddie while he greeted the crowd. He looked dazzling in his white suit and everything about him was polished. I was well into my 40s by now, so I was hardly what you might call a young rock fan, but Freddie stole the show, he was just fantastic. The crowd were screaming and cheering throughout his performance and you could feel his energy vibrating through the stadium.

I was buzzing with excitement as I walked back to the hospitality area and soon afterwards Freddie came. He looked tired but relaxed and I asked him what he would like to drink.

"Just some water please," he replied.

I wasn't surprised that he needed a nice cool glass of water after jumping around like that on stage!

One of the other highlights for me was watching as Phil Collins got into a helicopter to fly to the USA. Phil was the only artist who was to perform at Live Aid in both London AND Philadelphia. After coming off stage at Wembley he rushed out of the stadium where a chopper was waiting to whisk him to the airport so that he could catch a Concorde flight to The States. He would later rush onstage in Philadelphia and do another show. It was an amazing feat and he was to travel with our very own Barry Cox from the Hard Rock. When Phil's stage show was coming to an end at Wembley, I asked Betty to cover my tables and I went outside to watch Phil go on his way. I'd never seen anybody catch a helicopter before – and certainly not for a historic flight like this! When I got outside there were crowds of people and we all cheered and waved as he dashed into the chopper before it lifted up and soared off into the blue sky. It was very exciting.

As the day progressed there were so many big stars coming in and out of the hospitality area that it was hard to keep up with them all. The BBC was conducting interviews in the corner, so it wasn't long before we started to become very busy. I spotted George Michael arriving and I went over to greet him and I asked him where he wanted to sit. He looked very handsome and his bright white teeth gleamed through his big smile. Then he threw his arms around me and gave me a great big kiss.

"Oh God – I am never going to wash my face again!" I joked.

Meanwhile there was a bit of a drama while The Who were on stage. Roger Daltrey was in full swing belting out *My Generation* when suddenly a fuse blew and cut the power.

It happened at the very moment when Roger was singing the line, 'Why don't you all fade...'.

There was a bit of a panic backstage and people were running up and down shouting.

"Quick! Quick – find an electrician!" they bellowed.

Thankfully the power was soon restored.

While we were working, the giant fishbowls on the bar were quickly filling up with money. I assumed people would throw in coins but pretty soon they were brimming with banknotes. When the stars arrived with their entourage we'd ask them if they wanted to make a donation and they responded magnificently. Some of the VIPs would pat their pockets and if they couldn't find any cash, they asked their assistants to go and get some. Pretty soon the giant fishbowls were stuffed full of cash, which must have run into tens of thousands of pounds. Due to the warm weather we had giant fans on the ceiling to try and keep things cool in the marquee tent. They were blowing cold air down onto the bar where the fishbowls were placed and soon the banknotes started to flutter about in the wind. There were £10 notes, £20 notes and even £50 notes getting caught in the breeze and swirling around. In the end, one of the staff went and found two big polished stones from somewhere and we used them to weigh down all the money!

It was 4am before I finally arrived home that night. I was tired but I was happy. Live Aid was watched on TV by a world-wide audience estimated at 1.9 billion people – and it raised around £150million (around $250million).

It had truly been the greatest show on Earth.

We had to dismantle the temporary Hard Rock at Wembley the next day and take everything back to Central London, but we were still buzzing while we did it. It had all been fantastic. A few days later we all received a letter from Bob Geldof to thank us for all our help.

It was a pleasure Bob, it was a pleasure…

15

FAREWELL
ISAAC...HELLO 90s

WITH the burgers sizzling and the French fries turning golden under the grill it was hard to keep track of all the VIPs who visited us in London. We'd become the No 1 place for celebrities to hang out and I'd sometimes be so busy at work that I wouldn't recognize a famous face...even if it belonged to one of the biggest movie stars on the planet. It sounds crazy but you get into the zone and all that matters is the customers at your own tables, so if somebody is sitting in another part of the restaurant, being looked after by a different waitress you might not spot them. This could sometimes lead to an amusing incident, like the time when Keith Richards turned up looking for his son and nobody recognized him. Keith saw the funny side and he dove down on his knees.

"Where's the f***ing party!" he yelled in mock anger.

On another occasion I was serving a group of American customers on Table One at Old Park Lane when one of them asked for directions to Harrods. His parents were in their 60s and they were a charming family who'd come to enjoy the tourist sights in London. While I was giving them directions I saw a woman and three men out of the corner of my eye who'd sat at a nearby table. Their waitress must have been a little busy elsewhere because they'd been left alone for a few moments. While I was talking to the Americans I felt a little tug on my dress. It was the woman on the other table trying to get my attention.

"Your waitress will be with you in a second," I reassured her.

The woman was very polite and she seemed to accept my explanation, but a few moments later while I was dealing with the bill for the Americans, I felt another little pull on my dress.

"I'm afraid you're not at my table, madam – but I'll make sure that somebody will be with you very shortly," I repeated.

I made a mental note to go and find somebody to serve them but it was a busy afternoon and we had the usual line of customers in a queue outside the restaurant, so I was keen to free up the table that the Americans were leaving behind. After they left I wandered off for a moment but when I returned the woman who'd tugged my uniform and her companions had moved onto the empty table, even though it was dirty and needed clearing. I guess they were keen to be served and they must have preferred the look of my table to the one where they had originally sat. The problem was that we had a policy that customers weren't allowed to be shown to a table until it had been fully cleared, in case they accidently leaned on any spilled drink or any items of food that had been left over.

"I'm very sorry but I'm afraid you can't sit at this table until it has been set," I explained to the woman and her companions.

I was weighing up what to do next when a felt a tap on my shoulder. It was one of the duty managers.

"It's okay Rita, you're talking to NICOLE KIDMAN and TOM CRUISE," he whispered to me out of the corner of his mouth.

Then the penny dropped.

Not only had we kept two of the biggest stars in the world waiting, but also I'd failed to recognize them!

"Christ, Rita! You'd better think on your feet here," I thought to myself.

I'd read somewhere that Tom had recently been filming over in Ireland.

"Jeez Tom – how was Ireland because I know that you were just over there?" I said, straight away.

Thankfully they saw the funny side and Tom gave me a great big smile.

"I had the best fish and chips in the world in Dingle Bay in Co Kerry," he replied with a huge grin that flashed his immaculate white teeth.

I also looked at Nicole properly for the first time and I saw that she was drop dead gorgeous and dressed in a beautiful outfit. I made sure that I gave them my full attention after that!

* * * * *

ISAAC had continued to be the heart and soul of everything that we did in London but sadly he bid us a fond farewell in 1988. The Hard Rock lived on but in many ways it was the end of an era.

When the rumors began to circulate that Isaac was thinking of selling up at first I refused to believe them. The Hard Rock seemed to be in his blood and we were flying so high that it never crossed my mind that he might leave. According to the press we were by now serving over 1,200 customers a day at our restaurant in Old Park Lane (and sometimes I can tell you it seemed like a hell of a lot more than that!). Our quirky cafe had grown to become a global brand and we'd welcomed an estimated eight million customers through our doors in London since we'd opened.

"That funny little restaurant has sold more food than any other of its size in history," said Isaac in a rare magazine interview in 1987.

"The McDonalds people have told us it's impossible to serve that many burgers off such a small grill. They want to know how we do it."

When I'd first met Isaac had been little more than a boy in his early 20s but by now he'd matured into one of the best business brains on the planet – and he'd done it in style.

"It's very difficult to be a practicing Hindu and a capitalist, but I try to put some of my spiritual beliefs into my business. I don't think God minds you making money as long as you spend it wisely," he said in another interview.

The rumors that he was thinking of moving on came to a head in July 1988 when some of our staff heard something about a possible deal between Hard Rock and a very large hospitality and entertainment company called Pleasurama. I hadn't paid much attention to the gossip so it felt like a bold of lightening has suddenly struck us. Surely we weren't going to be saying farewell to Isaac?

A day or two later all the staff were asked to gather in London for a formal meeting. I felt sad because I realized that Isaac was probably coming to say goodbye to us. There was a tense atmosphere in the restaurant where about seventy or eighty of us were sat down waiting for him. When Isaac came in he had Maureen at his side and he seemed very calm.

"It's true that I have sold up," he confirmed.

He didn't say a great deal more and I can't remember much: I guess I was too shocked to listen. Afterwards he said a personal goodbye to some of the older waitresses like me, who'd been there since the beginning.

I can't recall his exact words but they were along the lines of: "Miss Rita, thank you for everything you have done. I am going to miss you."

I thought of all the crazy times we'd enjoyed together and I shed a quiet tear. I wasn't just saying goodbye to my boss; he was my friend too. I thought about how far we'd come together. Isaac had by now opened Hard Rocks in places that included not just London, New York and Dallas, but all over the world. Meanwhile, Peter Morton had followed up his restaurant in Los Angeles by opening Hard Rocks in cities west of the Mississippi including San Francisco and Chicago.

According to a press report in The Times in London, Pleasurama were paying £63million (about $100million) for Isaac's company, Hard Rock International Ltd. The tabloids speculated that Isaac's share of the deal was worth about £20million (around $32million). On the other side of The Atlantic, Peter Morton remained in control of Hard Rock America Inc. This meant that for a while there were two unconnected companies that controlled the Hard Rock name: Peter's company in the western United States, and Pleasurama, who had the famous restaurateur Robert Earl on its board (Pleasurama later briefly merged with a company called Mecca before they were taken over by The Rank Organization, which became our owner during the 90s).

I missed Isaac a great deal but he had one last parting gesture for me.

A few months after he left I was working in the restaurant just before Christmas when we received a phone call out of the blue. I was serving customers on the tables when somebody came to find me.

"Rita – it's Isaac on the phone and he says he wants to speak with you," they explained.

I went to take the call, wondering what Isaac could possibly want.

"Miss Rita, what time do you finish? Can you come around to my house, I have something for you?"

"Oh, I can't come now, Isaac. I am on the restaurant floor. I can come at 6:30pm?" I replied.

"No, that's too late. Maureen and I are flying to Dallas tonight. Ok listen. I will send a car for you tomorrow morning and I will leave an envelope here for you."

I thanked Isaac and I hung up wondering what he had in mind. The next day the car collected me and took me to his home, which was a grand Gothic looking building in Mayfair with wrought iron gates and a cobbled drive. As the vehicle whisked me inside I had no idea what to expect. A friend of Isaac greeted me and gave me a bulky envelope. When I looked inside I was staggered. It was full of cash. There was more money than I had ever seen in my life.

"Oh my God – I can't take this," I spluttered in disbelief.

"Rita – Isaac has given it to you," his pal explained.

I asked the friend to call Isaac in America. It was the middle of the night in Dallas but I knew he'd be up late as usual.

"Isaac, you're very kind but I can't accept this money. It's too much," I said.

"Miss Rita, this money is for you. I want you to have it," he replied.

I pondered what to do.

"Can I share it with some of the girls at the Hard Rock?" I suggested.

"Miss Rita, it is for you and you can do whatever you want to with it."

I thanked Isaac and we chatted for a while. He told me that he was feeling well and that he was very much in love with Maureen. Afterwards I walked back to the Hard Rock in a bit of daze with the envelope full of money in my handbag. When I arrived I went into one of the toilets downstairs and closed the door.

My heart was thumping as I counted out the cash.

There were lots of £50 notes (each worth about $80). I can't remember the exact total, but from memory there was more than the £1,000 ($1,600) he'd given me the time that I'd gone to Ireland. It was a typically generous gesture from Isaac but I didn't feel happy accepting the full amount for myself – after all I wasn't the only one who'd worked hard to make the Hard Rock a success. I called together three of the other old time waitresses who were working that day.

"Girls, Isaac has given me some money and I want to share it with you," I explained to the girls, who were all equally gob-smacked and delighted!

It was Isaac's parting thank you and it was a wonderful gesture just before Christmas. Isaac and Maureen were married in a dream ceremony in Monte Carlo the following spring. Maureen was the shining light in his life. Sadly, she passed away from leukemia in 1994.

* * * * *

WHEN Isaac sold his stake in the Hard Rock Cafe it was as if we had come of age because we were now officially part of a big corporation. Our new owners had plans for further expansion and Robert Earl was a bit of genius. I got on very well with Robert and he always impressed me with his ability to remember the name of everybody that he met. He was a very hard worker and the Americans loved him. Robert later caused a lot of noise by opening the first Planet Hollywood restaurant. Some of the newspapers in London saw Planet Hollywood as our competition and they ran headlines about 'Burger Wars' (I thought there was plenty of room for both of us!).

I remember one funny incident when I was in Orlando in around 1990. I was in the restaurant when somebody tapped me on the shoulder. I looked around and it was a very large security man.

"The boss wants to see you upstairs," he said.

I presumed he was talking about Robert Earl so I followed him up to the mezzanine. I got a surprise because it turned out that 'the boss' that the security man was referring to was in fact Steven Spielberg!

"You served me a few weeks ago in London," he smiled.

Steven sat surrounded by bags full of gifted Hard Rock merchandise and asked me if I wanted anything. I declined but we had a nice chat and he was a lovely gentleman.

Our 20th anniversary in 1991 was a wonderful time for me because it also marked my 50th birthday and the Hard Rock laid on a special surprise. We were owned by The Rank Organization by now and we decided to celebrate the anniversary by going back to our original menu from 1971 – complete with original prices. It meant that a burger meal was just 50p (about 80 cents) compared with a normal price then of £4.95 (about $8). The customers loved it and we had a queue around the block that was bigger than ever!

There was a lot of press interest in the anniversary and one of the newspapers asked to celebrate the occasion by taking a photograph of me. I'd been due a day off but I went into work especially on a Friday afternoon to have my photo taken. When I arrived the photographer was still tinkering with his lights.

"I hope it doesn't take too long, I'm to meet some friends later," I explained to the duty manager at the time, who was a young woman called Maggie.

"Don't worry Rita just take a seat," she told me.

Suddenly a glass of champagne appeared from nowhere.

"This is for you," she said.

I thought it was very strange because you'd never normally drink if you were about to meet the press, but Maggie insisted – and she even brought me a second glass afterwards. I was wondering what the hell was going on when four young guys walked into the room. They were members of the pop band, Curiosity Killed The Cat, who were flying high at the time.

They walked wheeling a big cake and came right up to my table. At first I didn't recognize them so I asked them who they were.

"You don't remember us, but we remember you Rita," they said. "You used to give us a free glass of coke when we didn't have any money. We're here to wish you a happy 50th birthday!"

The Hard Rock had laid on lunch with the band as a special surprise. The lads were on great form and they kept reminding me of all the times when they'd come into the Hard Rock when they were penniless musicians before they made the big time. I'd often sneaked them the odd free dish with Isaac's permission when they were down on their luck. Now they were rich and famous and they were here to say thank you! When our meal finished, the boys said they had one last surprise.

"We need you to come to Piccadilly Circus with us but when we get there you will need to wear a blindfold," they explained.

It sounded crazy, but what the hell! A car collected us we drove the short journey to our destination (I'd given up on the idea of meeting my friends by now). I was still wondering what the hell was happening when we gathered together at the statue of Eros in the middle of Piccadilly Circus, right in front of the giant electronic billboards that light up the night with their brilliant colors.

"Now Rita, no peeping," I was told, as the blindfold was placed around my face. After a short pause they spun me round and allowed me to take off the blindfold.

When I opened my eyes I was staggered.

The giant building in front of me was illuminated by a message in moving lights that read: 'HAPPY 50TH BIRTHDAY, RITA!'

It was the Hard Rock's way of wishing me a great time. When I'd first come to London as a young woman I'd always been fascinated by the bright lights at Piccadilly Circus and I'd written home to my mother to tell her about them. To have my own name up there was a wonderful gesture that I'll never forget.

We also had a 20th birthday party for the Hard Rock and I seem to remember that several VIPs from Rank turned up wearing suits. They were a lovely group but they were all dressed so formally that I couldn't help thinking that they looked slightly out of place.

"Come on guys, this is the Hard Rock! Take off those ties and put on some T-shirts," I urged them.

They were happy to agree and I even managed to persuade them to help out around the restaurant by taking iced water and drinks to the customers. I don't think they'd encountered too many bossy waitresses like me but they loved it. I soon had them charging around in Hard Rock T-shirts while they helped out on the tables and had fun.

Looking back, the 90s were another period of big expansion for us under the ownership of Rank. By 1996, there were 41 Hard Rocks operated by Rank (15 were company owned restaurants and 26 were franchises). Over in America, Peter Morton meanwhile owned 13 restaurants and four restaurant franchises. In June 1996, almost on the exact date of our 25th anniversary, Rank struck a deal with Peter Morton that made the financial world sit up and gawp. Rank paid $410million (about £250million) to buy Peter's restaurants. It meant that Rank were now in control of all of the 58 Hard Rock Cafe sites that existed around the world at the time. I was pleased that we were unified again as one company but I was surprised that Peter had agreed to the deal, so I called him on the telephone to ask why he decided to sell up.

"Miss Rita – they offered me a price that I couldn't say no to," he explained.

Business experts at the time estimated that the combined value of the Hard Rock could be close to $1billion (£625million). Not bad for something that began as a crazy little fast food joint that most people believed wouldn't stand the test of time.

Our 25th birthday was also a special time for me personally, because the Hard Rock was about to offer me a new role, which I'll tell you about in the next chapter…

16

HARD ROCK ATTACHÉ: RITA GOES GLOBAL!

MY job today involves travelling all over the world to meet the wonderful staff employed by the Hard Rock – and it seems like everywhere I go they greet me with a smile. In a funny sort of way, being a fiery Irish redhead who loves to chatter and talk makes me the ideal candidate for the job! I have a roving role that I've been doing since 1996 as part of my duties as Hard Rock Cafe's international Cultural Ambassador. My position means that I am lucky enough to attend all our grand openings as well as getting to meet and greet lots of famous people. I often get to arrive at the grand openings in a 60s white Cadillac! To me, the biggest VIPs are always our own hard-working employees, because they're the ones who make it all happen. Everybody in the organization has an important role to play, from the most junior member of staff right up to our current CEO Hamish Dodds, a wonderful man who I respect immensely.

The secret of our success is that we're a family and we look after our own. We demand enthusiasm and hard work from every member of the team, but the rewards that we offer in return are rich. Nothing gives me more pleasure when I travel around the different countries than to see young members of staff rise up the ladder and build great careers at the Hard

Rock. I always tell new recruits that it's a special place to work. Whether you stay for a week or forty years I like to think that some of the Hard Rock magic will rub off on you and it will stay with you for life.

I spent 25 years waiting on tables full time at the Hard Rock and I never got tired of the job or thought about looking for something new. When I was offered my ambassadorial role it came as a bolt from the blue at our 25th Anniversary party at the Hard Rock Cafe in London in June 1992. It was a wild night and everyone was determined to celebrate. We'd thrown open our doors to a glittering guest list that included stars like Sylvester Stallone, George Harrison, the singer Paul Young and Bob Geldof's lovely wife Paula Yates (who is sadly no longer with us). We were also joined that night by lots of senior people from our owners back then at Rank, including our CEO at the time, who was a good guy called Jim Burke. Most of the guests were gathered downstairs in what used to be our old basement (we'd converted it into a nice spacious part of the restaurant a few years earlier). We had a big birthday cake at the party that we planned to cut at midnight and as the clock ticked towards the big moment everyone was in great spirits. I was waiting on my tables as usual and I was on my way to the bar to collect a tray of drinks when I heard somebody shouting my name above the noise of the crowd.

"Rita! Rita! Come here – I've got something to tell you."

I looked up and saw that it was the CEO who had a big smile on his face. He was stood with one of his fellow directors near the bar enjoying the fun. I walked over and said hello.

"Rita, from midnight, you are off the floor," Jim said.

I watched as he pointed up to a clock on the wall. I could see the hands were ticking away and there was just a minute to go until the Hard Rock Cafe reached its 25th birthday.

"From midnight you have a new role," Jim bellowed. "We want you to travel the world and inject the spirit of rock 'n' roll and the Hard Rock everywhere that you go."

I was puzzled and I didn't quite know what to say. In truth, I was a bit confused and didn't know what he meant. Midnight arrived a few seconds later and everyone continued to get swept up in spirit of the party. I don't remember Jim saying too much more about it that evening. I think that amid all the noise and the fun I was too busy serving customers to really give it a great deal of thought.

It wasn't until I went into the Hard Rock a day or two later that I realized he'd been deadly serious about me taking on a new job. Not only that, but the whole world seemed to know about it!

"Rita have you seen the newspaper this morning?" somebody asked me when I arrived for work that day.

"No, why?" I replied.

"It says you've got a new job. It's written in the paper."

Surely not, I thought. I assumed they were mistaken until I was passed a copy of the Daily Express and there it was in black and white. I can't remember the exact wording but the headline said something along the lines of:

'WAITRESS TO BECOME HARD ROCK'S CULTURAL ATTACHE!'

I was truly flabbergasted. It was only a short article of about five or six sentences but it named me and explained that I'd been working at the Hard Rock in London since 1971. It went on to say that I'd been given a new role that involved helping to spread the Hard Rock's ethos and culture around the world. It all sounded terribly exciting – but I was more than a bit confused!

"Oh My God – I haven't even said I'll take it yet," I thought to myself.

There wasn't very much that I could tell my colleagues about the announcement but later on Jim Burke explained to me that Steve Routhier would be flying to the UK to tell me more about the role. Steve was the member of staff who I'd previously met in New York when he was cataloguing our memorabilia collection. He had the Hard Rock in his heart and I had fond memories of how he'd worked as a greeter at our New York opening back in 1984. He had long curly hair and he would sit barefoot outside the Hard Rock casually handing out menus with warm hippy-like charm. Steve had come a long way since those days and he'd even once been tipped as a future CEO. He played an important role in developing the Hard Rock brand around the world. When he flew into the UK a few weeks later we sat down together in the Hard Rock's office in London.

I like Steve a lot. He is an intelligent guy and he used his knowledge of rock 'n' roll well to become our Senior Creative Consultant.

"Rita – how do you feel about the new job?" he asked me.

"Yeah, I'm sure I am going to love it, Steve – but I'd like to know a bit more about it before I make a final decision," I explained.

Steve explained that it was a unique chance to become the Hard Rock's ambassador around the globe. It would involve attending all our grand opening and conferences whilst also greeting VIPs. A major part of the role would be connecting with our own staff to share with them the pioneering spirit that made the Hard Rock such a success back in 1971.

"We want you to spread the Hard Rock ethos to all corners of the globe," Steve explained.

I was flattered but I explained that I would miss being a waitress on the restaurant floor.

"In that case, why don't you continue to do a couple of days waitressing every week and we will send for you when we need you?" suggested Steve.

It sounded like a dream role and it came at just the right time for me. My children were grown up by now which meant that I had the freedom to travel. I'd also made a big change in my personal life several years earlier: Tony and I had got divorced. We remained good friends and we were still in constant contact with each other. The divorce had been an agonizing decision for me because Tony was still a good man (not to mention the father of my children), but he always put drink before our marriage. When I decided to stay at the Hard Rock all those years ago rather than rejoin Tony in Ireland I had finally realized we were never going to work things out. I was worried that his lifestyle would mean that we might lose our properties in Ireland so I consulted a solicitor, who explained that the best course of action was for me to file for a divorce. Thankfully, the split was amicable and I received one of the properties, while Tony continued to live in our main house in Ireland. It was a heart-breaking step for me to take and being Catholic it wasn't something that I entered into lightly. In fact, it turned out to be for the best because Tony and I continued to enjoy a lot of each other's company and he regularly came over to England for long periods to stay with me. It was the best of both worlds because we had our own space but our friendship remained intact.

I'd already done a lot of travelling with the Hard Rock; my time in New York had been just a start. I'd followed up by attending openings and helping to train staff in Europe and across America. I always get a huge buzz from meeting with staff in different countries. I find that wherever I go people seem to be fascinated by my story, they are amazed that I've been at the Hard Rock since day one.

The new ambassadorial role that Steve Routhier outlined to me was a golden opportunity and I readily accepted it. My family and friends were delighted for me and Tony had some kind words when I discussed it with him.

"Rita, I am very proud of you. I hope you enjoy every moment," he told me.

* * * * *

WHEN we open a new restaurant these days we always stage a grand ceremony and we usually celebrate by smashing a guitar or two on the front steps. For every one that we break we donate at least another one to a local charity. It's always an exciting moment but now that I'm a bit older it can sometimes be quite an effort to smash a sturdy Fender guitar. I just put on my hard hat and give it a good whack, which normally does the trick! In case you are wondering, the guitars that we smash have slight faults so they would otherwise simply go to waste. My job also involves attending all our staff conferences around the world, plus I get to welcome artists on stage at our live events like Hard Rock Calling.

I am lucky to work for great people today like our CEO Hamish, who always throws his arms around me and gives me a kiss! He's a charming Scotsman who was previously an executive at Pepsi before joining us in 2004. I first met Hamish when I spotted him at a staff conference in Miami and I bounded over to say hello.

"Oh you must be Rita," he said with smile.

I was flattered that he had taken the time to find out about my background. Hamish is a lovely mixture of being friendly and approachable, whilst at the same time maintaining the calm air of authority that a good CEO needs. I was very impressed by the first speech he gave us after he joined. Hamish made it clear he was in for the long haul and he told us that he intended to put his children through college by making a success of his time at the Hard Rock! He's done an amazing job and I often hear him talking about the importance of our staff – a sentiment close to my own heart.

I am also very lucky to work closely with our European Marketing Director in London – a handsome young Irishman called Marc Carey. He's the person who always calls to tell me when I need to travel abroad. The schedule can sometimes be grueling and involve long arduous journeys but I don't care one bit. When that telephone rings and Marc is on the line to tell me about a new assignment my heart always skips a beat. Suddenly I feel 20 years younger (and two stone lighter!) and I am happy to hit the road. During a recent trip to Marseilles in France I was so delighted when we were greeted at the airport that I burst into song and performed a little ditty in the arrivals lounge. Poor Marc didn't know where to look!

When I arrive at an airport there's often a member of staff there to meet me, wearing a Hard Rock baseball cap or T-shirt.

As soon as I see that famous logo I get a warm feeling and there's a smile on my face.

One of the reasons that the Hard Rock seems like one big family is that we are always willing to promote within the organization. Two of our vice presidents, Calum MacPherson and David Pellow, are great guys who worked their way up the company. Calum began as a busboy who worked alongside me when I was waitressing. Meanwhile David began as a general manager in Edinburgh. There are also countless managers and other senior staff who started their careers as waiters or kitchen staff. This means that they have a great understanding of how the business works. They're also a great inspiration for new recruits who join us at a junior level.

I am happy to say that my duties also involve telling customers about the history of the Hard Rock. Steve suggested that I should set aside a regular day to do this, so on the first Thursday of every month we started to host what was called our 'Lovely Rita Day' (I was very flattered by the title!). I would spend the afternoon on the restaurant floor mingling with the customers and telling them all about our past. I enjoyed it immensely and the customers seemed to love it too because pretty soon there were crowds of American tourists who would arrive every month with their cameras around their necks. They were fascinated by the story of the Hard Rock and they loved to hear all about the early days in London.

* * * * *

I DECIDED that the best way to approach my role as cultural ambassador was to be my ordinary self. I'm plain-speaking Rita and being open and honest with people has served me well over the years. One of my first big assignments was to fly to Atlantic City to meet the tycoon Donald Trump at a grand opening for a new Hard Rock at his Taj Mahal hotel and casino.

"God only knows what a big billionaire like Donald Trump will make of straight-talking waitress like me!" I wondered.

It all seemed a bit unreal but I'd become used to meeting important people over the years and I decided that I'd just have to take it all into my stride. I flew to LaGuardia airport in New York where I was due to catch a shuttle flight onto Atlantic City, but when I arrived there Hard Rock told me there had been a change in my travel arrangements. Instead of flying to Atlantic City they laid on a car to take me there. When I went outside to the pick up point there was a big black stretch limo waiting for me. It had blacked-out windows and inside it was enormous – it seemed like it was almost as big as my apartment in London. There were leather seats and champagne and I felt like a rock star! I normally travelled to work by bus in London. I would have been just as happy to catch a bus ride in America, but I must admit I appreciated all the comfort. When we arrived at Atlantic City we were in an area that seemed very run-down back then (although I'm sure it's improved today). As I looked out of the window the streets looked very dreary and empty, which was not what I'd expected at all. Then we turned a corner and suddenly it seemed like we'd arrived in a paradise. There were grand buildings and bright lights everywhere. I felt as if I'd just arrived in Disneyland!

When I checked into the hotel I noticed that there seemed to be hundreds of wealthy-looking older people in the casino. They were all busily playing away on the slot machines. I was shown up to my room where I saw a strange-looking bath in the corner.

"What's that?" I asked the guy from the hotel.

"That's a Jacuzzi, ma'am," he explained.

"Oh," I replied. I'd never seen one before.

Later that night I met with the staff from the Hard Rock and we ran through the plans for the big event. The next morning when I went back down into the hotel I walked through the casino and I was astonished to see all the old people were still there, glued to the slots. I wondered if some of them had been up all night. More and more guests seemed to be arriving outside by the busload.

"Mr. Trump will be arriving at the Hard Rock via the red carpet at around 10am," a colleague told me.

The plan was that I would be part of the group that would greet him before we went on stage at the Hard Rock to give a short speech. I was waiting in line when a gentleman in a suit came up to me.

"He won't shake your hand," he said to me sternly.

I was a bit surprised to say the least.

"Why not?" I asked.

"Because of germs," he replied.

These days it's been widely reported on the Internet that Mr. Trump has a germ phobia, but it wasn't something that I was aware of back then, so I couldn't understand why he didn't want to touch me.

"OK that's fine… alright," I replied.

When Trump arrived he was wearing a beautiful suit and he looked smaller than I imagined he would be. I felt awkward at not being able to greet him with a handshake, but I gave him my best smile.

"Hi, I am Rita from the Hard Rock. I know you won't shake my hand but follow me in," I said when I met him.

Then without really thinking about it, I lifted my arm up to give him a pat on the back. I meant it as a warm gesture but it actually felt like I gave him a bit of a whack!

He just gave a brief laugh and I don't remember him saying anything to me at that point. My first impression was that he wasn't very interested in talking.

"This is all very strange," I thought to myself.

The event was packed with VIPs including the local mayor and I think there was even somebody there from the White House. Jim Burke went on stage and made a speech on behalf of the Hard Rock, during which he explained how happy we were to be in Atlantic City. I sat in the audience and listened proudly to what Jim had to say. Next it was Donald Trump's turn to speak and he stood up and made a very brief address. I was expecting to go on stage later on after the mayor had spoken but when Trump finished I suddenly heard Jim calling my name.

"Where's Rita?" he asked.

"Oh God, I've got to go up there now!" I thought.

I raised my hand and I was ushered onto the stage. It seemed like there were hundreds of TV cameras there but it all happened so quickly that I didn't have time to pause before I addressed the audience, who had spent the last 20 minutes listening to a billionaire and a CEO. I swallowed nervously and decided to hope for the best.

"Well, you've heard just it from the big guys," I began. "Now you are going to get it from the horse's mouth! I'm Rita from the Hard Rock and I am honored to be here in this fine city of yours today..."

My speech wasn't as polished as Jim or Donald Trump had been when they had spoken, but I gave it to the audience from my heart and afterwards people raised their hands to ask me questions from the floor. They wanted to know all about the Hard Rock's history and also about our plans in Atlantic City. When my session on stage came to an end I was amazed to receive a huge clap and a standing ovation.

I walked over to Donald Trump and I couldn't resist giving him a cheeky wink.

"You see what I am getting – you didn't get any of this," I joked.

My comment seemed to make Trump warm to me. He broke out into a great big smile and he came over and put his arms around me. The cameras flashed and a photo of us together later made the front pages. He was very nice to me afterwards and I realized that he hadn't meant any disrespect by refusing to shake hands. In fact, he turned out to be a real gentleman and he wanted to know all about my work at the Hard Rock. We chatted for a long time and he offered to arrange a tour of the area for me.

"Do you want to go anywhere in the city? I will make the arrangements," he said.

"Oh thank you, but I am just here to see our staff, " I explained.

He was charming to me, absolutely lovely. It just goes to show that your first impressions can sometimes be so misleading...

17

JOY FROM THE QUEEN: SADNESS AT HOME

I'VE always believed that if you work hard and help others you will be rewarded in life – but I never expected that it would win me a medal from The Queen! I was very honored when Buckingham Palace announced that I was to receive an MBE in 1998 for services to the tourism industry. I was working away in Germany when I found out and my jaw nearly hit the floor. In fact, when I woke up in my hotel room the next morning I thought it had all been just a dream! But when the news sank in I was very proud, because in my eyes it was Royal recognition of what the Hard Rock has done for the hospitality industry, not just in the UK but also around the world. The Hard Rock allows you to be yourself and we value everybody as equals. It's an ethos that lots of other companies now adopt but I am proud to say that we were the first.

To this day I'm not sure who nominated me to receive the award but I assume it was somebody senior at the Rank organization. I had no idea that my name had been put forward and I was busily meeting and greeting businessmen at a trade fair in Berlin when a call came through from the Hard Rock in London to tell me about it. A male colleague answered the mobile phone that we had under the counter at the event and he passed it to me. The call was from one of our general managers back in the UK.

"Rita – you have got to come home right now. You are going to be honored by Her Majesty The Queen," he explained excitedly.

"What do you mean?" I spluttered. "There must be a mistake, what would The Queen want with me!"

I listened while the caller explained that the officials at Buckingham Palace had already written to me at my home address in London. They were concerned because they hadn't received a reply, so they'd contacted the Hard Rock. I hadn't seen the letter so it must have arrived while I was away travelling.

When the call ended I was in a daze.

"What exactly is an MBE?" I asked the young colleague who'd handed me the mobile phone.

He explained that it was a formal medal from The Queen's Honours List and a great privilege that is only bestowed on very few people.

"It's one of the highest honors that she can give to a civilian," he said.

I was gob-smacked! While we were talking word spread around the trade fair like wildfire. Within a few moments it seemed like there were hundreds of German and American VIPs all gathered around me to offer me their congratulations. I was still working and I had my uniform and name badge on, but pretty soon the champagne corks were popping and people kept coming over to ask me to pose for photographs.

The next day I had a breakfast meeting with one of our marketing executives – a lovely German girl called Kirsten. The night before was a bit of a blur and I genuinely wasn't sure if I'd imagined the whole thing.

"Kirsten, I think I had a strange dream last night," I said.

"It wasn't a dream, Rita. It's really going to happen, " she smiled. "Everybody will be waiting for you later on at the conference center to congratulate you," Kirsten added.

When we arrived somebody placed a big Stetson hat on my head and the crowd gave me a cheer. Later that morning I rang Tony to tell him the news. Even though we were divorced we continued to maintain our close friendship and I would always call him whenever I was away on business. When I told him about the MBE his kind words almost brought tears to my eyes.

"Rita, you have made me so very proud, I am delighted for you and all that you have achieved," he told me.

The Hard Rock were keen for me to fly back to London, but as far as I was concerned I still had a job to do in Berlin.

"Oh no, I'm not leaving – this is rock and roll and the show must go on!" I insisted.

I continued to give it 100% at the trade fair and it wasn't until two days later that I got back to London. When I arrived at work all the girls on the restaurant floor were laughing and they greeted me with great big smiles. They were proud because they knew that the award was a seal of Royal approval for the Hard Rock.

I was to be presented with the MBE a few weeks later at a special ceremony at the Hard Rock by a government minister. Even though the award comes from The Queen, she doesn't present them all in person. Because I am Irish (rather than a

British citizen) my MBE was technically an 'honorary award', which meant I didn't need to go Buckingham Palace to receive it. I didn't mind because the Hard Rock is my home and I was happy to receive it there.

I had one more nice surprise in store before the big day, because the Hard Rock laid on a dream holiday for me as a way of showing their appreciation. I was sent off to Villa D'Este, a beautiful 16th Century estate on Lake Como in Italy, with my daughter Tara. It's a grand hotel and when we got there I thought it was the most beautiful place in the world. There were orange trees in the grounds and the building was a magnificent sight, with polished marble floors and huge pillars. I arrived wearing a Marks & Spencer dress but after we checked in, Tara took a look around and came running back to tell me we'd need to dress in our best outfits.

"Mum, you better put another dress on. They are all wearing outfits that look like they were bought from Harrods!" she laughed.

We had a wonderful, relaxing stay but by the time my presentation ceremony arrived a few weeks later I must admit that I was very nervous. In fact I was shaking in the car on the way to the Hard Rock that morning. I wore my white wait-ress uniform, onto which I proudly attached a selection of my favorite pin badges. After nearly three decades of watching rock stars and celebrities making grand entrances, today I was the one who was to arrive on the red carpet – and I must admit that it felt very strange. I've always considered myself to be just another waitress at heart so part of me kept wondering why I'd been chosen for the award. Then I would remind myself that it was for the Hard Rock, not just for me. There were lots of press photographers invited to the ceremony, at which the Culture Secretary, Chris Smith, presented me with the medal on behalf of The Queen. I received it on the same stage where Paul McCartney had performed at the Hard Rock in the 70s.

"Rita has given outstanding service to tourism through her work at the Hard Rock Cafe," Mr. Smith told the audience.

"She is renowned for combining efficient service and a lively approach to the job. Over the years she has been deluged by letters of thanks from her customers."

It's been a pleasure, I thought.

The medal itself is very beautiful and I still treasure it! Afterwards I posed for photographs and it seemed like every newspaper in England and Ireland wanted to talk to me. The headline in the Daily Express the next day made me smile. It said:

'ROCKING RITA IS SERVED UP AN MBE'

It was a wonderful day. I didn't get to meet The Queen, but I did bump into Prince Andrew's ex-wife Fergie a few months later while I was working at an MTV event in Rotterdam. Fergie was there as a guest and was sat down chatting with Anjelica Houston and Jerry Hall in our hospitality area. I occasionally wear my MBE on special occasions and Fergie spotted it on my lapel.

"Oh well done. Congratulations – isn't my mother-in-law lovely?" she said to me. I thought it was cute that she referred to The Queen as her mother-in-law.

"Oh I didn't get to meet The Queen. My award is an honorary one," I explained.

Fergie was delightful to talk to and I told her about the time that I had served princesses Beatrice and Eugenie. Fergie was very approachable and when I asked her what she wanted to drink her answer surprised me.

"Oh I'll just a have a coke but don't worry. I will get it," she said, and she stood up and got her own drink.

Nowadays I don't wear the actual MBE medal very often but I have a small replica that I can use for special functions. Getting the copy made was Bob Geldof's suggestion after he spotted me in the Hard Rock one day.

"Where's your MBE?" he asked. "You know that you can get a miniature one made to wear in public?" he said.

Bob had been presented with an honorary knighthood for his charity work and he'd had a copy made of that.

Looking back, the day that I received my MBE is one of my happiest memories. There was only one tinge of sadness on the day itself, due to the fact that Tony wasn't able to attend. I would have loved for him to have been there to see it all but he was unwell. His drinking was beginning to take a toll on his health and he had taken a fall. Unfortunately, I would soon discover that things were about to go from bad to worse in that respect.

* * * * *

I'VE always believed that my husband Tony was a good man at heart but his weakness was that he refused to get any help for his drinking until it was too late. I sometimes wonder what my life would be like now if he were still here today. He was a charming man but he had his own secrets, some of which I guess I may never know. He was a wonderful talker but he was a slave to the drink. During our marriage he was rarely there for me. Instead he preferred to go off for hours on end to the pub. But there were also occasions when he could be the nicest man on Earth and I loved him very much as a person. Sometimes on a Saturday morning he would go off to Selfridges and spend £200 on expensive food and return to our flat in a black taxi stuffed full of shopping bags. I remember one Christmas he stayed in bed long into the afternoon to sleep off the booze, before walking into the lounge in his dressing gown.

"I don't suppose you bought us a present," my daughter asked him sadly.

"As a matter of fact I did," replied Tony. "I have bought you a gift that will bring a smile to your face," he added, beaming with delight.

Tony then produced two very expensive toothbrushes and two tubes of toothpaste, which cost £8.50 each (which was a lot of money at the time). It made me smile because Tony always had beautiful teeth.

Strangely, after we divorced our friendship continued to blossom. We both loved our three wonderful children and at times the divorce seemed like nothing more than a piece of paper. In my mind he was still my husband, even though we could choose to be apart whenever we wanted.

Sometimes my job means that I can be travelling solidly for a couple of weeks, but Tony was always the first person I would call. I'd also try to visit a local church, where I'd find a quiet moment to say a small prayer (which is something that I still do today). One of the most epic journeys that I ever made consisted of a tour of South Asia and Australia and it was while I was away that Tony's health rapidly deteriorated.

My travel schedule started with a flight to Singapore after which I was due to fly onwards to meet our staff in Bali, Bangkok, Jakarta and Kuala Lumpur. Then following a brief return to Singapore I was due in Australia where I would visit our Hard Rock venues in Melbourne, Surfers Paradise and Sydney. The whole trip was due to last about twelve days, which meant that I'd be flying back-to-back every day.

I was very excited by the prospect of the trip but I was worried about how Tony would get on while I was away. He hadn't been feeling his old self and sometimes he wouldn't eat, especially if there was booze to be had instead. Tony's mother had passed away a few months earlier and he was planning to spend a few days tidying up business at her old home, in a small village in Northern Ireland called Newtownstewart in Co Tyrone. Before I caught the flight to Singapore I asked my daughter Tara to go and stay with him for a few days during the early part of my trip, after which she had to go home to the UK. I'd then catch up with Tony after I got back, which meant that he'd only be alone for a few days.

"Can you make sure he gets a bit of dinner every day," I asked Tara before I left.

My flight from London to Singapore lasted 16 hours but it was like relaxing at The Ritz while I was on the plane. The girls from Singapore Airlines looked every bit as immaculate when we arrived as they did when we set first off! The trip was a fantastic experience and I met some wonderful people on my travels. It made me realize that the Hard Rock is truly famous around the globe and I was very proud. Apart from a small hitch with my visa (which nearly stopped me getting into Australia) everything went according to plan. I kept in touch with Tony as best as I could and when I arrived back in London I was exhausted but happy. I planned to go and see Tony in Ireland the following week so on the Monday evening I gave him a call.

"Hi Tony, how are you? I will be in Newtownstewart to join you on Friday," I explained.

He insisted that he was OK but he was muttering and I could tell that he'd been drinking all day. I realized that I wasn't going to get much sense out of him while he was under the influence so I promised to call him back in the morning. Then, as I put down the phone, I got an uneasy feeling.

Something's wrong.

It's hard to explain but I just knew something was up. It was a bit like the time that I knew my workmate was pregnant without being told. Perhaps I'm a little bit psychic or maybe it's just feminine intuition. I tried calling Tony back but there was no answer.

"Maybe he's gone out for more drink," I thought.

There were three pubs in the village and when I called the first one the landlady told me that Tony had been there earlier.

"Oh, he was drinking all day and he was dancing but he was fine. He's not here now but try calling next door he might be in there," the publican's wife suggested.

I rang the second pub but they told me that Tony wasn't there either, so I asked if they could send somebody around to his mother's house, which was close by.

"I'm a little bit bothered because I just keep getting feelings that something is not right, " I explained. "Could one of your lads go and check on him for me?"

"Of course we will, Rita. Don't worry – we're sure everything will be fine," the landlady told me in a calm and reassuring voice.

I arranged to call them back in twenty minutes but instead ten minutes later – much sooner than expected – my phone rang again. It was the landlady's son.

"Rita, we have just called an ambulance!" he said.

I listened in shock while he explained that Tony had been found slumped and in a daze. My intuition had been right – something was very wrong.

Tara was back in the UK by now so I caught the next flight to Belfast at 6am the following morning. It was a three-hour bus ride down a dusty old road to Newtownstewart. When I finally arrived at the hospital the nurses at first refused to let me see the doctor, but I insisted they let me through.

"Tony is my husband and the doctor WILL talk to me," I told them.

When they eventually agreed, the doctor explained that Tony had cirrhosis of the liver.

"He is not very well," the doctor said. "But you can go and see him."

Tony was groggy and his skin was a yellow color but he seemed to be okay. I was thankful that he was able to sit up in bed to speak to me.

"Hello Rita – I hope that Australia treated you well," Tony said. His voice was weak but I could hear the old charm in it.

The next few days settled into a strange routine during which I lived in a small room at the hospital, which had a kettle and a hard chair but not much else. Tara was in the UK and I didn't want to stay alone in an empty house. Besides I wanted to be at the hospital to care for Tony. Each morning I would go to the canteen to fetch him boiled eggs and porridge, which I would then feed to him. I did my best to make him comfortable. The hospital had lovely gardens of dark green grass and sometimes I would take Tony outside in a wheelchair to enjoy the view. I hoped with all my heart that he was getting better and that he would be allowed home soon.

I was due to go to Amsterdam the following week in order to join a children's function at the Hard Rock and I knew that if I was still going to attend that I would need to book my flight. I was in two minds: I didn't want to let the Hard Rock down but there was no way I was leaving my husband if he needed me.

Tony died on the following Friday.

It was a terrible shock. I tried to feed him as normal that morning but he didn't eat anything because he felt too weak. The nurses had removed some tubes from his bladder the day before to see if his body could function on its own. He looked very sick but I had no idea that he was dying, nobody told me. Tony managed to sit up in his wheelchair but after a while he needed to sleep.

"Rita, please put me back into bed," he whispered.

When I popped back to see him a little later he asked me to give him another blanket.

"I am cold Rita, you know," he said.

I covered him up and I went for a walk around the hospital, during which I called the Hard Rock from a pay phone on the wall.

"Rita, we need to make a decision about Amsterdam. We'll check the flights and call you back," the girl in the office told me.

When she rang back I'd just picked up the phone when a nurse came walking over.

"Oh, there you are," said the nurse.

"Hold on a moment, I've just got to answer this call," I replied.

The nurse didn't give any indication that it was urgent so I carried on talking on the phone, but after a while I realized that she was waiting for me. I rang off and I gave the nurse a smile.

"He hasn't taken a turn for the worse has he?" I joked, not realizing that the situation was serious.

Then I linked arms with her in a friendly manner and we walked back to Tony's room. When we arrived there were two other nurses waiting by his bed. Then the penny dropped and for one awful moment it felt as if the world had stopped spinning.

I'd only been gone for less than ten minutes but Tony now looked completely different. He had bloated up in size and he was very pale. His eyes were closed and I immediately knew that the worst was about to happen.

"He's not going to go, is he?" I said in a panic.

The nurses nodded.

"What now!!" I cried.

I wasn't prepared for this but without thinking I leaned forward and I pulled him close to me and I hugged him tight. Tony died in my arms. While he passed away I kept talking to him because they say the hearing is the last sense to go.

"Tony we love you...you were the best father in the world...Tony we love you...we all love you so much," I whispered to him, rocking him backwards and forwards and repeating the same words over and over again.

He was 52.

I miss him dearly to this day. He is always in my thoughts.

Isaac had moved on, he kept in touch and occasionally he would come into the restaurant to see us all. It was on one of his surprise visits that the subject of the vault came up.

I was still getting over the death of Tony at the time. The loss of my husband had left me feeling terribly sad and it was a great help to have the support of my family and all my friends the Hard Rock to help me through it. Tony had always said that he one day wanted *My Way* by Frank Sinatra to be played at his funeral along with *Imagine* by John Lennon. When I asked the priest he refused because he didn't think it was appropriate for inside a church. But Tony got his wish because my daughter arranged for both pieces of music to be played outside the Church while his coffin was taken to be buried. It was a fitting send-off of which Tony would have approved. I could imagine him smiling down on us from Heaven.

I was working in the restaurant many months later when Isaac arrived unannounced. I didn't serve him but I saw him come in and he looked just like his old self with those striking blue eyes.

"How are you, Miss Rita?" he beamed, flinging his arms around me when I went over to say hello.

We chatted and he said how sorry he was to hear about Tony. I gave me a lift to see Isaac in good spirits because to me it felt like he was still part of the family. He'll always be part of the family. While he was in town, Isaac got chatting with some of the guys from Rank and told them that he'd heard that the building next door that housed Coutts & Co was up for sale.

I don't know exactly what he said but it was along the lines of: "You should buy it and open a shop there to sell Hard Rock merchandise. The customers will love it."

It was a clever idea that was typical of Isaac. He always thought on a grand scale. He wanted the biggest and the best. And when you think about it, where better to store our treasure than The Queen's bank vault? After all if it was good enough for Royalty it's good enough for our wonderful guitars and outfits.

Our executives at Rank must have loved the idea because they acquired the lease on the building and in March 2001, three months before our 30th anniversary, we opened our rock shop with the vault below it. I can still remember the tingle of excitement as I visited the vault for the first time. As you descend the staircase the noise and bustle from upstairs fades to silence. The doors are made from steel nearly two feet thick and on the front of them you call still see The Queen's crest of royal appointment.

Once inside, you are surrounded by treasure. On your right as you go through the huge metal doors you'll find a red coat with a black furry collar and furry cuffs that once belonged to Elvis Presley. The King of Rock and Roll wore the coat back in 1974, according to a sign on the wall. Dotted around the room there are over 20 electric guitars, all of which belonged to rock gods including Jimi Hendrix, Jimmy Page and Jeff Beck. Hendrix's guitar is a custom-made 'Flying V' Gibson left-handed model and it is the last guitar that he played onstage before his death. Meanwhile, one of my favorites is Keith Richards' famous red ESP electric guitar, which has small burn marks on the top of the neck where he used to clip his cigarette whilst playing on stage (there's a photo alongside it to prove it!).

There are also hand-written lyrics by John Lennon and a 'Beatles Corner' where you can see the original piano from Abbey Road studios, on which the band recorded *All You Need*

Is Love and *Lucy In The Sky With Diamonds*. If you take a stroll further around the vault you'll find a bench with cushions where visitors are sometimes allowed to sit and pose for photos. The bench originally belonged to Hendrix. There also items belonging to icons like David Bowie, Adam Clayton, Sting and Slash. Another piece of memorabilia close by that always gets a lot of attention is Madonna's white bustier that she wore during her Blond Ambition tour during 1990.

* * * * *

WITH so much history behind the restaurant and the vault it's no surprise that people come to visit us from all over the world, but I was amazed by a request that I received one day in my role as cultural attaché. I took a phone call from a man in Chicago who had an unusual request.

"I am coming to London and I want to get married at the Hard Rock," he told me.

At first I thought he meant that he wanted to hold a wedding party in the restaurant, but the gentleman explained that he and his wife were in the Guinness Book of Records for taking their wedding vows the most number of times. They wanted to add the Hard Rock to the places where they'd held a marriage ceremony. It sounded like a great idea to me.

"Yes, that's fine. Come in and have lunch and then get married!" I agreed.

Unfortunately, the manager of the restaurant had different ideas when I told her about it.

"Oh no Rita, we can't do that. We don't have a license for it," she explained.

I was worried because I'd already told the gentleman every-thing would be fine. Luckily the man who was overseeing our vault at the time stepped in to help.

"We can do it in the vault, " he suggested. "I'll arrange a special spiritual blessing there for which we won't need a license."

It sounded like a great idea and I was very honored when the couple asked me to be their bridesmaid. On the big day I wore my white waitress's uniform that was decorated by all my favorite pins from the Hard Rock and I was carrying a big bouquet of flowers. The couple loved it – and we even threw in a free wedding cake, champagne and lunch at the Hard Rock.

Now that's what you call great service! They still write to me every Christmas and they have now been married over 100 times.

* * * * *

THE historic rock 'n' roll items that we have on display in London are magnificent, but they're actually just a small part of Hard Rock's world-wide collection of music memorabilia, which is by far the biggest of its kind. If you walk into any Hard Rock around the world you'll normally find wonderful items on display. In fact, whenever we plan the opening of a new restaurant it normally takes between 300 or 400 pieces of treasure to decorate it in the style that our customers love. Our collection now includes around 75,000 items worldwide and lots of them can be viewed on the Internet. Many of them are also cataloged in an excellent book called *Treasures of the Hard Rock* written by Paul Grushkin and Joel Selvin with my friend Steve Routhier. It's a great read and when it was released I sat down with Paul and Joel and we signed 500 copies together in one go! The authors say that a rock 'n' roll museum should be somewhere between a cathedral and a whorehouse – and that the Hard Rock manages to be somewhere in the middle! I'm not sure that I'd choose to phrase it quite like that, but I guess what they mean is that the Hard Rock is a temple where people come to worship their icons – but at the same time it's wild and wonderful. If you're a musician then having your guitar in the Hard Rock has become a mark of your success, which is why we constantly update our collection (the newest addition to our vault in London at the time of writing is an acoustic guitar belonging to Imagine Dragons).

One of the reasons our collection is so extensive is that for many years after Peter and Isaac went their separate ways, they both continued to collect vast quantities of items for their respective Hard Rock businesses on different sides of the world. Brian Murphy and Steve Routhier scoured the world attending auctions for Isaac, while Peter's collection was put together mainly by a guy called Warren Stone (who was the brother to Peter's first wife, Paulene).

In 1986, Routhier spent a quarter of a million dollars in just four hours at Sotheby's buying dozens of signed albums, photographs and other valuable items. Among the items that were purchased by the two Hard Rock companies over the years was Elvis Presley's 'shooting star' jump suit, which went for £28,500 (about $47,000). Michael Jackson's leather jacket from the cover of the Bad album was snapped up for £20,000 ($32,000) and Buddy Holly's horn rim glasses were bought for £26,000 (about $42,000). Many other items were donated or simply brought into the Hard Rock by private individuals. The haul apparently even includes an old tooth of Madonna's found stored in an old box of her belongings. According to an article in the Daily Mail published in London during September of 1988, the Hard Rock had invested over £8million ($13million) in rock memorabilia by that date. When Peter sold up to Rank in 1990, his collection was unified with the one that Isaac had acquired. Nobody knows quite what the collection is worth in today's money because not only is it so vast but many of the items are literally priceless (what would YOU pay for Madonna's old tooth)!

A vast amount of our collection is stored in Orlando where our global headquarters are located. The Hard Rock Cafe in that city is the biggest in the world and it is described as being like a Roman Coliseum of Rock. It has more memorabilia than any other location, with a vast multi-level cafe and live music area with room for 3,000 people. Tucked away in an inner confine it also has it's own private 'Lennon Room' devoted entirely to John Lennon. It's one of my favorite places and everything inside it is connected to the late Beatle. When you step inside you are walking on carpet that was once in his home and the room is decorated with furniture that came from the Manhattan apartment where John and Yoko once lived. There are cups that he once drank from and a pair of the glasses that he wore. The room is amazing and when you are in there you can feel his presence.

It's magical.

* * * * *

THERE'S a funny story about our memorabilia collection that Pete Townshend once told me – and it still makes me chuckle today. Following the huge success of our grand opening in New York in 1984, the next big city that Isaac set his sights on was Dallas. He was determined that when the Hard Rock hit Texas we'd take things to even bigger heights – which meant Steve Routhier was in charge of sourcing a whole mountain of additional memorabilia.

"Miss Rita – you won't believe our plans for Dallas," Isaac told me.

The new restaurant was going to be opened in a former church that Isaac had acquired and which he planned to convert into his own cathedral of rock 'n' roll. It was a fabulous old building with 18-foot alcoves that illuminated the interior. Isaac decided to install the Hard Rock's own stained-glass windows, each of which would celebrate a rock 'n' roll icon. Elvis Presley was in the middle with Chuck Berry to his left and Jerry Lee Lewis to his right.

Isaac poured many millions into getting the look and feel of the place exactly how he wanted it – and outside he even installed a giant grasshopper-style oil pump with a huge arm that moved up and down.

"If it's pumpin', we're open!" a sign explained.

When Isaac's old friend Pete Townshend got to hear about the plans for Dallas he was only too happy to help.

"When you open that up I want a brick from my front room inside the place," Townshend apparently told him.

Isaac loved the idea of a little part of Pete's home being among the attractions in the building. Townshend owned a gigantic old house in the countryside and I assume that Isaac must have duly arranged for somebody to go and collect the necessary materials. When the Dallas restaurant opened it was truly magnificent. The green room was decorated just like Townshend's English country mansion, complete with wooden paneling and beams across the ceiling.

It was only many years later that I discovered that Pete had actually donated far more than he had originally expected. We met while we were both in Miami when Pete came to talk to the press in a private room. When he arrived he appeared a little down and I got the impression that he wasn't in the mood to talk to reporters. When his manager told him I was there his face brightened up and he came over to say hello.

"It's great to see you Pete," I said. "I have a T-shirt that I want you to sign for charity if that's okay," I asked.

Pete was happy to oblige and afterwards we had a few photos taken together while we chatted about old times.

"Do you remember when we took a brick from your front room to add to our Dallas restaurant," I asked him.

Pete's eyes lit up.

"Yes I do," he replied. "You were only supposed to take a brick but you ended up taking the whole f***ing lounge without me knowing!"

Apparently, he only found out afterwards. The idea of somebody carting off Pete's living room to the Hard Rock made me laugh aloud.

"Oh well, back then you were probably too stoned to notice!" I joked (of course Pete is always clean and sober these days).

19

FIRE AT THE HARD ROCK!

I WAS enjoying a quiet weekend at home in London when I received a telephone call from a colleague that filled my heart with dread.

"Rita – there's been a fire at the Hard Rock," she told me.

I felt the air suck out of my chest: a fire is every restaurant's worst nightmare.

"Oh my God, has anybody been hurt? What happened?" I stammered.

I listened in horror while my distraught workmate told me that the restaurant had gone up in smoke at noon on a busy Saturday while we were getting ready to welcome hundreds of customers. The building was still on fire and there were flames inside the kitchen that were licking up from the ground floor towards the roof.

We have strict procedures for how to cope with an emergency at the Hard Rock – and the first priority is always to get the customers and staff out to safety. We'd had to evacuate the restaurant many times over the years but it was usually for a false alarm, this was the real thing. In a situation like this you need to be blunt – you tell the customers to get out quick and you follow them outside. There's a Royal Mail pillar-box on the corner near the restaurant, which is where we would assemble outside during any problems. The kitchen is always the obvious place for a fire to start in a busy restaurant.

"Are the chefs okay, did you get everybody out?" I asked.

"Yes Rita, we think that we managed to get everybody out but there is still smoke billowing everywhere and the fire engines are here."

I was feeling sick inside and I said a silent prayer to God, hoping that it was correct that there had been no injuries. The date was July 9th 2005 and the Hard Rock had been my home for nearly 25 years. The thought that everything we'd worked so hard for might have been destroyed was too terrible to contemplate. I knew I had to go straight into work immediately.

"I am coming in now. I'll be there as soon as I can," I told my colleague.

I was petrified of what lay ahead while I was on the bus. It had been a very tough few days in London. Two days earlier the city had suffered its own version of the 9/11 terror attacks. Terrorists had set off four bombs on the transport system, killing 52 people and injuring over 700 hundred during what become known as the 7/7 attacks. For two days the TV screens had been filled with horrific images of suffering.

As my bus pulled alongside Hyde Park I was anxious to get off and walk the rest of the way as quickly as I could. My spirits dropped when I saw a cloud of dark smoke hanging in the distance. When I finally arrived the building was cordoned off and there were half a dozen fire engines outside. There were crowds of people milling around trying to find out what was going on. Thankfully the blaze itself had been extinguished, but the firemen were still dousing everything down to make sure it was safe. The BBC later said the fireman had done a magnificent job, especially as they'd been at full stretch for two days dealing with the aftermath of the bombings. I hugged my workmates and I was relieved when it was confirmed that nobody had been hurt. There were only a few customers inside when the fire broke out because we'd only just opened. It had started with a small blaze in the kitchen so there had been enough time to get everybody outside.

I went home that night with mixed emotions. I was relieved that nobody had been killed but I was worried about what we would find when we were allowed back inside the building. When I came in on Monday morning I was shocked by the damage. Our beautiful restaurant was black and smelly and damp. It reeked of smoke and there was dirty water and soot everywhere. Most of the damage had been caused by the smoke and the water from the fire hoses. I looked at the famous bar where so many icons like Eric Clapton and Pete Townshend had stood over the years. It was empty and black. It felt like all we were left with was a dark shell.

"Oh my God," I said to myself.

In fact, the damage wasn't as bad as it might have been because the fireman had managed to put the fire out very quickly and the building itself was fine. Amazingly, they'd also managed to save most of the rock treasures that were on display in the restaurant. Eric and Pete's guitars had been carried outside and had survived! Of course, everything in the memorabilia vault was safe and sound anyway because it's across the road and surrounded with two feet of steel. Pretty soon, we began to realize that things weren't as bad as they had seemed. Our mood began to lift.

"We're gonna clean this place up and have a big re-opening party," one of the managers told me.

I couldn't have agreed more. In fact, there was no doubt for even one second that we wouldn't open again as soon as possible.

"This is the Hard Rock – let's get it rocking again," I said to my workmates.

I grabbed a mop and bucket and for the next two weeks that's what we did. We were joined by specialist cleaners and we worked around the clock until every inch of the place was spotless. Bit by bit the restaurant was restored to its old glory. The smell of smoke was gone and everything was gleaming.

It was actually the second time that the place had survived a fire because there had also been a blaze in January 1988, although that had been a far smaller fire. It occurred in the early hours of the morning while there were 200 customers in the restaurant but everybody had been led outside. The Sun newspaper ran an article the next day stating that our gold record collection and memorabilia collection had been undamaged. I also remember the Evening Standard publishing a piece that said that even though the Hard Rock was on fire people were still trying to line up to come inside!

For me, the clean-up effort after the 2005 fire was a great example of the spirit of the Hard Rock in action. Everybody pulled together and worked as a team to turn around a tough situation. It was hard work but that never scared any of us and a few weeks later we hosted our reopening party. The place was packed with happy customers and celebrity guests. Apparently Michael Jackson was in town at the time and decided to drop by. When he arrived, the place was so busy with crowds of people inside that his management changed their minds and decided to go somewhere quieter!

* * * * *

THE fire came in the middle of a very hectic time because in the weeks that preceded the blaze we'd been involved in Live 8, a massive rock event that Bob Geldof organized to commemorate 20 years since Live Aid. I was also getting ready to go off later in the year to New York, where we were relocating our Hard Rock Cafe from 57th Street to Broadway near Times Square.

I had fond memories of Live Aid so I sat up and listened when Bob announced plans for an anniversary event to coincide with the leaders of the G8 visiting the UK in early July. Live Aid had been the biggest show on Earth and in my mind they'd never be able to duplicate it, but Bob was determined to prove everybody wrong. His plans for Live 8 included over 1000 musicians around the world who would be performing at several different sites, including London and Philadelphia.

The London part of the event was being held right on the doorstep of the Hard Rock in Hyde Park. The line-up of stars included lots of great names from the original event like Sir Paul McCartney, Bono and Madonna. They were joined by younger musicians like Robbie Williams and Coldplay, who were only children at the time of the original Live Aid gig (Robbie Williams is one of my personal favorites and I have met him several times!). It was an impressive line-up and the scale was even bigger than the original Wembley event, with 120,000 people expected to pack into Hyde Park. There would also be events in all the G8 states and in South Africa, with everything kicking off in Japan. The Hard Rock was naturally involved and with Hyde Park being so close to our restaurant things would hopefully be a little easier to organize than they had been at Wembley, plus we were trusted old hands after all!

Geldof had gathered everybody together the previous autumn to record a new version of the charity single *Do They Know It's Christmas?* – and I was very honored when the Hard Rock asked me to go along to the studio. The song was recorded in Hampstead in North London. All the big stars were there plus lots of new ones from the UK, like Will Young and Joss Stone. Will is a lovely guy and I'd enjoyed watching him on TV when he won *Pop Idol*, the show that Simon Cowell appeared on prior to *The X Factor*. Will is very down to earth and he was lovely to talk to when I served him an orange juice.

"Rita – I used to be a waiter and I absolutely loved my job," he told me.

When I met Bob Geldof he shook my hand warmly when we met and we posed for some publicity photos together. I'd got to know him well since Live Aid and I had many fond memories of him popping into the hard Rock. He could sometimes be a moody fella and often wouldn't look up while he was ordering, but underneath his tough exterior he had a warm Irish charm. He'd come into the Hard Rock with his wife Paula (who died tragically in September 2000).

Back in the day, Bob would always ask for herbal tea, even though I'd told him many times that we didn't have any on the menu back then.

"What herbal tea have you got, Rita?" he'd ask.

"We've got normal Typhoo and you know that's it," I'd reply, wagging my finger.

When I met him at the recoding session in Hampstead, Bob had all his children there with him, including Peaches (who has also sadly passed away now). Bob presented a video news report from 20 years earlier that showed a small child who'd been caught up in the famine in Ethiopia. It was a very harrowing piece of footage. The girl was only about three years old and she was suffering from severe starvation. She had a ghostly face with sunken eyes and she was obviously close to death.

I was sat very near to Bob and as the video played I noticed that he quietly started to cry. The he looked up and addressed the room with tears running down his cheeks.

"Do you see this child? In 1985 when this video was filmed she had ten minutes to live," he said.

It was so silent that you could have heard a pin drop in the room while Bob spoke.

The girl in question was Birhan Woldu, whose face had been flashed around the world in 1985 during Live Aid. She'd become a powerful symbol of the suffering in Africa when a nurse had said that she was very close to death. But miraculously Birhan had survived and what's more I knew that she was going to be there with us in Hampstead.

"Well she didn't die," continued Bob. "And she is here with us today."

There wasn't a dry eye in the place as Birhan joined Bob on stage. It was hard to believe that she had once been so close to death. In front of me was a tall intelligent woman who spoke five different languages and had a degree in agriculture. When you see somebody who has turned his or her life around like that it is very humbling. It was a very special moment and I am proud that the Hard Rock had been part of both Live Aid and Live 8.

The 2005 concert was a success. The crowd on the day seemed more like 250,000 people than the original estimate of 120,000. Bob Geldof invited me backstage and I had a fantastic time watching some of the acts. One of the highlights was when Birhan went on stage and she triumphantly held hands with Madonna. The picture of them standing side by side with their arms in the air said it all.

Bob did an amazing job and I find it so sad that he's encountered so much tragedy in his life. It had been a terrible shock for him when Paula Yates died in tragic circumstances from an overdose. Bob and Paula were estranged by then but it obviously still hit him hard. I was terribly sad too because I had fond memories of chatting to Paula in the Hard Rock. Her two eldest daughters, Fifi and Peaches would help out around the restaurant by offering to tap my orders into the machine after we became computerized in London. When Fifi was about to turn 18, I received a phone call from Bob,

"Rita, we're having a party for Fifi at the Hard Rock and I'd like you to be there because I know she thinks a lot of you," he said.

I told Bob I'd be delighted and we had a great time. Fifi was full of energy and spirit on that night and they packed out the Hard Rock with their friends.

When Peaches died from on overdose in 2014 it was too painful for words. My heart went out to Bob and his family.

* * * * *

ONE of our greatest ever grand openings came about a month after Live 8 when we relocated in New York. The restaurant that we'd opened in 1984 on 57th Street had been our home in the Big Apple for 21 years. It was in a good location just around the corner from Carnegie Hall, but in 2005 we'd come of age and we set our sights on moving to Times Square. The Hard Rock acquired the iconic Paramount building on Broadway that was big enough to house a brand new restaurant and an 1800 sq.ft. Rock Shop for all our merchandise.

The Hard Rock was keen for me to be there for the opening of the new restaurant.

"Rita, the new site is unbelievable and we want you to help with the grand opening. We've got some fantastic plans," a member of our team told me.

I had fond memories of being part of our first restaurant on New York back in 1984, so I knew that I would be sad to bid farewell to the old place. I thought about all the fun and chaos that Eve and I had enjoyed while we mixed with the likes of Dan Aykroyd and Eddie Murphy. I wondered what my colleagues in New York had in mind to celebrate the opening of the new Hard Rock.

Our restaurant in London had only just reopened for business after the fire when I started making plans to fly to New York, where the opening ceremony was due to take place on August 12. When I arrived in the city I sat down with the Hard Rock team to run through the plans for the big day, which included organizing the world's biggest guitar smash.

"Rita, we are going to smash 100 Gibson guitars in a special ceremony to mark the occasion," they told me.

I was to be one of a group of people doing the smashing along with our CEO Hamish Dodds. We were to be joined by Brian Wilson of the Beach Boys and Steven Van Zandt from

Bruce Springsteen's E Street Band. When the big day arrived there was an amazing carnival atmosphere in New York. There were crowds on the streets cheering and waving the Stars and Stripes. Steven Van Zandt was to collect a final piece of memorabilia from our old restaurant on 57th Street and then ride off in an armored car surrounded by a cavalcade of Harley Davidsons, which would make its way to Broadway. When the procession arrived, I was to greet Steven on the red carpet and escort him to a stage area where we'd begin the ceremony. I was intrigued to meet Steven (or 'Little Stevie' as his friends call him) because I'm a big fan of *The Sopranos*, in which he played the famous Mafia character with the big hair, Silvio.

The crowds on Broadway weren't sure exactly who was going to be in the armored car so when it pulled up and the door opened there was a big cheer of delight when Stevie stepped out. At first I didn't recognize him because he doesn't have Silvio's hairstyle in real life – in fact he was wearing a purple bandana. But then I saw his smile and I recognized him immediately. He came over and put his arm around me and gave me a kiss on the cheek.

"Hello Steven – we're going to smash some guitars," I said.

"Let's do it," he replied.

Steven had a lovely warm manner about him. I felt very comfortable talking to him and we've now become friends over the years.

We wore protective glasses on stage and swung the guitars against concrete blocks to smash them. For every one that we broke the Hard Rock donated another one to a youth charity called Peace Games. It was hard work and in front of us there was a huge dumpster to collect up all the broken bits. The crowd loved the spectacle and soon people were clamoring to take home pieces of the guitars as souvenirs! I also received a lovely souvenir that day because Steven turned to me with a broken handle in his arms.

"Do you want this one, Rita?" he asked with a big wide smile.

Normally we are not allowed to take home anything like that but on this occasion I was given permission to keep the smashed up bits of Stevie's guitar, which I later got framed.

It had been a busy summer with Live 8 and the fire in London, plus the grand opening in New York. Looking back, Live 8 was an important event for us because it took place in Hyde Park. Little did I know at the time, but the following year we'd be holding our own huge live rock event on the same site...

20

THE HARD ROCK CELEBRATES 40 YEARS!

IT was one of those glorious summer mornings in London when the sun gently rises into a clear blue sky and bathes the city in crisp golden light. It was still very early in the day so the hum of the traffic in Park Lane was much lighter than usual and the air smelled fresh and clean. I was about to spend the day with 80,000 people at a gigantic musical event. The Hard Rock was due to host our very own rock festival in Hyde Park. There would be no Bob Geldof around this time to organize everything, but I wasn't worried. After three and a half decades in the business I was confident that we'd make a huge success of things. Besides, my immediate boss and good friend Marc Carey had spent many months tearing his hair out to ensure everything ran smoothly (God bless him)!

The date was July 1st 2006 and our annual event known around the world as Hard Rock Calling was about to born (although at the time it was initially referred to as 'Hyde Park Calling'). The lineup of stars about to blast it out onstage included some of the biggest names in rock, both old and new. Roger Waters was to perform Pink Floyd's *Dark Side of the Moon* in its entirety featuring Pink Floyd drummer Nick Mason, while The Who headlined on Sunday. The bill also included greats acts like Razorlight, Texas, Starsailor, The Lightening Seeds, Primal Scream, The Zutons and Suzanne Vega. In addition to the public, there would also be hundreds of our own staff present. Every single Hard Rock around the world had invited two or three members of staff along in order to share in the occasion.

My own role was to welcome our overseas staff to London and to tell them a little bit about our proud history. Later on I was also to introduce some of the great artists on stage. It would be a long day and my work probably wouldn't end until long after the last act finished at around 10:30pm – but who cares about sleeping when you can be hard rocking?

I wanted to make an early start so I'd spent the previous night at the Metropolitan Hotel, which is a short walk away in Mayfair. I was joined by a lovely young lady called Meredith from Coyne, our New York based PR company.

When I reached the gates to the park the security was already very tight, but thankfully there was a little buggy waiting to whisk us inside. When Meredith and I arrived backstage it seemed like there was a whole village of trailers for stars to use as dressing rooms. There's a rule that that the artists are not to be disturbed when they are in their own private quarters, especially before they are due to perform.

As Meredith and I walked the final few yards towards our first staff meeting of the day I suddenly heard a man shouting my name.

"Hey Rita! Rita – over here," he called.

I looked towards the direction of the voice but the sunshine was splitting through the trees and the haze temporarily dazzled me. I couldn't see who it was, so I just gave him a friendly wave and carried on walking.

"Hold on a minute," said Meredith. "That's Pete Townshend!"

I squinted against the sun and sure enough it was Pete. He was standing at the entrance of his trailer with a big grin on his face.

"Come on Rita, come over here and have a drink!" he yelled.

That is typical Pete. He's a true trooper and when he's in the mood he loves to have a good chinwag about the old days. The Who were top of the bill for the entire event that day, but Pete didn't have any false airs or graces. He just wanted a bit of company.

"I can't join you – I'm going to work," I called back.

"Oh come on – just come over for one," he insisted.

"Not now, I am busy. I will come and find you later on," I promised.

It reminded me of when Tony Curtis used to pester me for a chat at work in the early days. Pete's long association with the Hard Rock made him the ideal person to help us promote the event in Hyde Park. The newspapers are always interested in him because he isn't afraid to speak his mind. The press had quoted Pete at our launch event as describing Pete Doherty (who was making headlines in London for his wild behavior) as 'the ultimate rock and roll f***wit'. But Pete also has a heart of gold and a share of the proceeds from the Hype Park event was to go to the charities that he champions. As for my relationship with him, there were no hard feelings about the fact that the Hard Rock had once 'borrowed' the entire contents of his lounge!

I never did get to share that drink with Pete later in the day because I was rushed off my feet the entire time – but Hyde Park Calling was a roaring success and The Who were fantastic.

The only small problem was that it was so hot that weekend that about 30 people had to be treated for heat exhaustion, but thankfully they were all okay.

* * * * *

THAT first event in Hyde Park was a trailblazer because it was the start of the preparations for our 40th anniversary. The Hard Rock had visions of hosting a huge rock festival in 2011 to celebrate our birthday and where better to stage it than just across the road in Hyde Park? There was no way that we were going to let such a magical anniversary pass by without having a giant party. In order to ensure that Hyde Park was available for 2011 we had to sign a contract six years in advance. One of the conditions of the contract was that we also had to stage events in the park from 2006 onwards (so you could say that it was the longest birthday party in history!).

The Hard Rock was delighted to secure the use of the park because having our own annual rock festival was a great opportunity to raise money for charity while also having a great time. We also used it as a way of regularly bonding with our staff from other countries. The plan was that every year, two or three hundred people who work at various Hard Rocks around the world would be invited to fly over to London to spend the week of the festival with us. We'd put them up in a hotel and give them a great time while they learned about our rock 'n' roll heritage. The scheme has been a great success and it's become one of the ways in which we say thank you to those members of staff who have gone the extra mile – plus it's a great opportunity to spread the culture of the Hard Rock.

Everybody normally gathers together in front of the stage on the first day of the festival before the park is open to the public. It's one of my favorite times because it's wonderful to see so many staff from different backgrounds, including lots of young waitresses and kitchen staff who are just starting careers with the Hard Rock. I'm usually asked to kick things off by saying a few words, which I'm very proud to do. I arrive by buggy and I wear my original white waitressing dress, which I decorate with all my pins from the Hard Rock and my MBE. I'm always amazed by the warmth and friendliness of our staff and I'm often flattered when they give me a big cheer!

I tell them: "Hiya guys! Thank you all for coming, we are going to have a great day, this is Hard Rock Calling. I'm here for you for three days – if you want to ask me anything, just come up and tap me on the shoulder!"

People are always fascinated so there's never any shortage of questions to be answered. Meanwhile, we've also had the privilege to host countless great acts over the years. Our headline names at Hard Rock Calling in June 2007 were Peter Gabriel and Aerosmith (somebody took a great photo of Steven Tyler giving me a cuddle!). The following year we welcomed Eric Clapton back to the Hard Rock to headline the first night of the festival, with The Police leading the line-up the following evening. Eric's live performance at Hard Rock Calling sticks in my mind because he played with such passion and spirit. I'd seen him play a few months earlier in Florida and on that occasion I thought that he seemed very flat and lacking in energy. In America he'd spent most of the time sitting down on a chair on stage and at the end he walked off after nodding a quick goodbye. But in London, Eric was back to his old self, singing every word of his wonderful songs like *Layla* with great emotion. I met him afterwards with Hamish and we congratulated Eric on his show and we posed for a few photos together.

Paul McCartney and Bruce Springsteen also played at Hard Rock Calling several times. I think Paul's mellowed out a great deal in later life, especially since the birth of his youngest daughter Beatrice, who'll be a teenager soon.

"Hiya Rita!" Paul says, before throwing his arms around me.

During one of my meetings with Paul, the Coyne agency wanted me to ask him if he'd be willing to sign a guitar for them.

"Of course I will Rita," he said, grabbing the pen.

Paul then wrote his signature across the guitar and pulled me close with the pen still held in his hand.

"Would you like me to write something on your face too!" he teased, with a big smile.

Springsteen is also a real character.

"Are you ready to rock, Rita?" he asked me.

We posed for a photo together at Hard Rock Calling and afterwards there was a headline about me in a newspaper that read along the lines of:

"I LOVE MY JOB – I GET TO PARTY WITH THE BOSS!"

I couldn't agree more. Over the years we've welcomed so many big acts to Hard Rock Calling that's impossible to mention them all here, but we're grateful to each and every one of them.

* * * * *

IT was at the end of 2006 that a very important event occurred in the history of the Hard Rock when the Seminole Tribe of

Florida became our new owners. Rank had been in charge of the Hard Rock since the 1990s and during that time we'd continued to grow around the world. By 2006 there were around 124 Hard Rock Cafes, four Hard Rock Hotels and two Hard Rock Live venues, plus of course our vast memorabilia collection. The entire group was sold for $965million (£510million). It was a breath-taking amount of money: nearly a billion dollars. Not bad for a company that started off with a single cafe in London that everybody thought would turn out to be a flop!

The Seminole Tribe are a Native American people with a proud history and a wonderful culture. They already owned the franchise to two Hard Rock hotels – and they operated several of their own casinos in Florida – which made them the ideal people to take over the Hard Rock when Rank decided to sell-up.

"This is a proud moment for the Seminole Tribe of Florida and for all Indian tribes," said Mitchell Cypress, Chairman of Tribal Council, at a press conference in December 2003.

The Seminole Tribe made it clear from the beginning that they intended for the Hard Rock to continue to grow and prosper.

"It is also an opportunity for the Seminole Tribe to diversify its business operations and to help a very successful company to achieve even greater growth," added Mitchell Cypress.

Later on I would get to meet James Billie (who we affectionately call Chief Billie), the current Chairman of the Tribal Council, at one of our events in London. I know he cares passionately about the Hard Rock – and he's also very close to Steven Van Zandt, so we have a mutual friend. I'm very pleased that the Hard Rock is in safe hands with the Seminole Tribe.

With the backing of our new owners, the Hard Rock continued to make plans for our 40th anniversary celebrations in 2011. Marc Carey sat down with me in London and explained that he wanted me to play a special role.

"Rita, we want to put you on the road to do a tour. It will involve going to various cities and talking to the media and our staff about your life with the Hard Rock – and celebrating 40 years," he said.

Marc is a great believer in the culture of the Hard Rock but he always says that it's very difficult to teach it to other people; instead it's something that you have to live and breathe. The Hard Rock is built on great characters with energy and enthusiasm. Marc felt the best way to convey that message was with a tour that would take in a dozen major Hard Rocks around Europe, plus a five-day trip to America.

"You'll also play a pivotal role at the Hard Rock Calling 40th anniversary event, talking to the staff and introducing the acts," Marc added.

It was a big undertaking but thankfully I didn't have to do it all at once because Marc suggested that we do things in stages. Besides, I'd become used to traveling around the world by now. It was always a pleasure to go to new places and meet new people. I've never had a problem with that, although sometimes I encounter the odd shock. I remember once being in the Far East many years ago (I won't say exactly where it was) when the hotel offered to cater for my every need. When I checked in the concierge told me that I had a sumptuous suite. I'd have been happy with an ordinary room, but later the hotel staff rang me and said they were keen to ensure everything was to my liking.

"If you would like, we can accommodate you madam," the man said.

"Oh no, my accommodation is fine thank you," I replied.

"No, no – I mean we can arrange to '*accommodate you*'," he repeated.

I didn't know what he meant so I shrugged it off, but later on when I came down to reception another member of staff repeated the offer.

"Can we accommodate you?" said the person on the desk.

It was only later on when I spoke to a colleague from Hard Rock that I leaned what the phrase meant. My colleague was shocked because apparently it was the local term for arranging for a man to come to your room to 'accommodate' your romantic needs. I had to laugh, but it certainly wasn't for me!

Thankfully, there were no shocks like that on the 40th anniversary tour. I had a fantastic time in Europe where I travelled around major cities visiting our restaurants. When the month of May arrived it was time for me to go off to the States, where I was to visit Los Angeles, San Antonio, New York and Chicago, before going down to our headquarters in Orlando. My fondest memories are of the celebrations that took place in New York and Chicago, where I attended fun events at baseball games in both cities. In New York, a birthday cake was presented to the Hard Rock, which I accepted on behalf of the company before a big game at the Yankee Stadium. They gave me a signed ball and a box containing some sacred grass from the pitch.

A few days later I had the honor of pitching the first ball of the season at Wrigley Field in Chicago, home of the famous Chicago Cubs. They serve the best hot dogs in the world in the pub opposite the stadium. I must admit that I was very nervous when they announced over the speakers to the crowd that I was the Hard Rock's original waitress. My heart was thumping as I stepped forward onto the field – once you have put your foot out there is no going back!

It was an amazing feeling to go out onto the pitch and be surrounded by the magnificent stadium on all four sides. The crowd were screaming and cheering and I could see myself on the big monitors in the stands. People were clapping and waving at me and I felt so flattered to be chosen to represent the Hard Rock on such a big occasion.

"My God – this is how David Beckham must feel," I thought to myself, while I held the ball in my hand.

I walked out to my spot on the field and I just stood there for a moment while I breathed in the ambience. What a magnificent experience! Then I pulled back my arm and I pitched the ball with all my might. I watched as it flew through the air and safely into the hands of the catcher. The crowd roared their approval, much to my relief! I was in my glory and it will always be one of my happiest memories.

After pitching the ball – my next task was to sing with the crowd. It's a tradition there that the crowd always sings the famous baseball song *Take Me Out To The Ball Game.* The same gentleman traditionally led the song on a microphone for many years before he passed away. Now each year they invite a special guest to sing it, and as an honor to Hard Rock, I was volunteered for the job! Our global Head of Marketing, who at the time was a lovely man called Brian Siemienas explained the importance of the song.

"Rita, you've got to learn the words because you're going to be singing in front of thousands of people," he said.

Learning lines is not my strongest point. Whenever I am on stage to introduce an act, I like to just be myself and I find it helps if I move about with the microphone and I just say what comes into my head. Learning a song would be slightly different but I was happy to give it my best shot.

"Don't worry – I'll do my best," I promised Brian.

If you're a baseball fan you'll know that the song includes a line that says, '*Buy me some peanuts and crackerjacks*'. There's also a section that goes, '*For it's one, two, three strikes you're out.*' In the days leading up to the event I had several practice sessions until I thought I had it right.

"Rita – have you learned the song yet?" Brian would ask me every time I saw him.

On the big day itself, after pitching the ball I went up into a small box in the stand where I took the microphone. Somebody had kindly put the words to the song on a piece of paper just in case I needed them, but the writing was very small and I had trouble reading it. I must admit that my heart was thumping. I was joined by a group of lads from Canada who had won our Battle of the Bands competition.

"Come on lads, you sing along behind me," I said.

When the stadium's famous organ started to play I took a deep breath and sang the first line. The crowd were wonderful and joined in immediately and thankfully I managed to get my lines right, although instead of singing '*one, two, three strikes you're out,*' I apparently actually said '*one, two, three balls and you're out.*'

It was a small error and nobody seemed to notice – or so I thought.

A day later a colleague came up to me and said it had caused a bit of fun on the radio.

"Rita – what's all this they are saying on the radio? Apparently you said 'penis and balls' during the song!"

It sounded crazy to me so I decided to ask Brian if he knew anything more about it. Brian went bright red.

"Who told you about that?" he asked.

When I told Brian somebody had heard it on the radio, he explained what had happened. Apparently a couple of commentators at the game had joked on air that when I sang 'peanuts', it sounded like I'd actually said 'PENIS'!

They'd obviously misheard because I would never use that word in public. I know that I said 'peanuts' – but I could see the funny side of it. I'd like to reassure all baseball fans that I'd never disrespect them in that way. Thankfully, it didn't cause any offense – but it gave a few people a bit of a smile!

Later that year I also had fantastic time in London at Hard Rock Calling. Marc Carey worked hard with our promoters Live Nation to make a big success of the 40th anniversary event, which ran over three days in June 2011. The headline acts were The Killers, Bon Jovi and Rod Stewart. I went on stage to introduce Rod to the crowd and I sang a few line of his song *Maggie May* to help everyone get into the party spirit!

There were two bars named after me at the event, one was called Lovely Rita's Tavern and the other was called Olde Rita's Arms. It made me so proud to have my name up there on the signs in the middle of Hyde Park. During the early evening I noticed a group of young Americans sat in the VIP area. They were cast members from the American TV series Glee. We were told they didn't want to be approached but I went up to say hello and they turned out to be lovely lads.

I said: "Hey guys there's a bar over there with my name on, why don't we go for a drink?"

They loved the idea and we ended up pulling pints behind the bar and making cocktails to drink together to celebrate.

Jon Bon Jovi caused a bit of a stir while he was in town by popping into the Hard Rock Cafe while a Bon Jovi tribute band were playing there. For a laugh we sneaked him into the bar and when the lads from the tribute band took a break for a drink he jumped out to surprise them. Their faces were a picture! They couldn't believe it was the real Jon Bon Jovi. Afterwards Jon took part in a jam session with them. It brought the house down.

Forty years of Hard Rocking is an amazing achievement... and as for the future, we'll just keep on rocking!

21

TEA WITH MR TWINING IN THE OLYMPIC PARK

YOU might think that it would be hard to top our 40th anniversary celebrations but in fact our Hard Rock Calling event has continued to grow. Some of my nicest memories are of when Hard Rock Calling was held at the Queen Elizabeth Olympic Park in London in 2013. We were the first company to stage an event at the park following the Olympic Games in 2012, so there was a huge amount of preparation to ensure everything went according to plan. It was also the first time we'd moved the event away from Hyde Park.

When it comes to rock 'n' roll you can't get everything right all of the time. I've got memories of hiccups that have occurred over the years. I can recall one occasion when Chuck Berry asked for some of his favorite cigarettes just before he was about to perform on stage. One of our staff gave him the wrong brand of cigarette and he looked so furious that I feared that he would refuse to sing. He had a few choice words to say about it, but I needn't have worried because Chuck is a great artist and moments later he was belting out *Johnny B Goode.*

There have only ever been two celebrities who declined to pose for a publicity photo when I've asked them. One was Chris Moyles, the former BBC Radio One DJ. He was having a cigarette at the time in between being on air and he politely explained that it was against the rules for him to pose for pictures, which I respected. The other person was Amy Winehouse. She'd been eating a meal with a bodyguard and some friends in our hospitality area and when she got up to leave one of our PR people suggested that I say hello to her. Amy was a darling to talk to and her eyes lit up when she saw all my Hard Rock pin badges.

"Oh I love your badges, my mum collects them," she told me.

Amy stood there admiring the pins but she said she was feeling tired and she didn't want to pose for a photo. I had no problem with that – in fact I felt a little guilty about asking. Amy seemed to have a slight sadness about her and I got the impression she'd have preferred to be left alone. It's so tragic that she died at such a young age. She was hugely talented and a lovely girl to talk to.

One thing that many people ask me about is whether or not anybody famous has refused to leave a tip whilst I was waitressing. I can't think of anybody apart from the pop group Abba, who I served many years ago. I didn't mind in the least – a tip should always be optional.

* * * * *

ONE of the biggest upsets I've ever witnessed occurred at Hard Rock Calling in 2012 when unfortunately somebody pulled the plug during the grand finale to the show. Bruce Springsteen was the headline act and he was in full flow on stage after being joined by Paul McCartney. The crowd were going wild at the sight of the two rock gods performing a surprise duet together – when suddenly all the power went dead and everything was plunged into silence.

I was sitting in the green room watching the show on a big TV screen when it went quiet and the stage lights were dimmed. At first I couldn't believe my eyes and ears. One minute ago I'd been enjoying listening to Springsteen and McCartney singing *Twist and Shout*, then suddenly nothing.

"Oh my God, there'll be hell to play if somebody has pulled the plug," I thought to myself.

There were over 76,000 people in the audience who'd paid good money to see the show – and it had been cut off in its prime because it was overrunning by about half an hour. Apparently, the council regulations stated that everybody had to be offstage by 10:30pm and it was nearly 11pm, which meant there was a risk of having to pay a heavy fine. Somebody had taken the decision to kill the power, but I was amazed that they didn't wait until the song ended. Bruce Springsteen had been thrilling the crowd for three hours and he was furious that the show had been spoiled during the final moments. He knew the cameras were on him and like a true professional he kept on strumming in silence, but the power cut spoiled everything.

Not surprisingly, the decision to pull the plug caused a huge row. Steven Van Zandt was alongside Bruce when it happened and he later vented his fury via Twitter.

"One of the greatest gigs ever. But seriously, when did England become a police state?" said Steven, who went on to accuse the killjoys of "f***ing with 80,000 people having a good time."

There was a huge storm in the press over the next few days and even the Mayor of London, Boris Johnson, publically said that he thought the show should have been allowed to continue until it ended.

"If they had called me, my answer would have been for them to jam in the name of the Lord," said Boris in a comment to a newspaper.

I agree with him. Music is the medicine of life and what more could you ask for in the shadow of Buckingham Palace but McCartney and The Boss! I'm sure The Queen would have approved (I know her grandchildren would have done because Prince Harry has been known to visit Hard Rock Calling).

The incident caused a lot of outrage but Springsteen later turned the tables and got his revenge in true rock 'n' roll style. He had the last laugh by poking fun at the killjoys at his next live gig, which was a week later in Dublin. Bruce went on stage and he held up a large power switch.

"Before we were so rudely interrupted," he explained to the crowd, flipping the switch to the 'on' position.

Springsteen then carried on singing *Twist And Shout*. Later on he held up a big sign that said:

"Only the Boss says when to pull the plug."

I never got to meet the person who actually switched off the power at Hard Rock Calling. I guess nobody was in a hurry to own up!

* * * * *

I'VE been very lucky to represent the Hard Rock at lots of charity events in recent years and it's always nice to see celebrities giving up their time for good causes. On one occasion I was asked to present a Silver Clef award to Ozzy Osbourne at a charitable function. I sat in the audience with Ozzy and his wife Sharon beforehand and we had a good chat. Their daughter Kelly was there too and I found them a nice family to talk to. Ozzy is quite a character and was excited about receiving his trophy.

"When am I going to get the award? I want to give it to my dad to put on the mantelpiece in Birmingham," he said.

I had the Silver Clef in my hand but we had to wait until we were called up in front of the audience.

"Not now, we've got to go on stage together," I explained.

When we were eventually called Ozzy seemed to take an age to come up onto the platform and he almost went to grab the award from my hand. We were supposed to say a few words before I handed it over and I had visions of us playing a tug of war.

"Just give me it!" he joked, before adding some colorful language. Thankfully his voice was out of range of the microphone! The Hard Rock's charity commitments have also taken me to some wonderful places, including inside No.10 Downing Street. Lady Jane Rayne, who is the patron of the ChickenShed Theatre Company, invited me to attend a charitable function there. Lady Rayne is a former Maid of Honour to The Queen and she's very approachable and friendly. Her daughter Natasha has done a lot of charity work with the Hard Rock and we've attended many functions together over the years. I didn't get to meet the Prime Minister on that day but his wife Samantha hosted the reception and she was interested to learn all about the Chicken Shed and its great work. Who'd have thought it – that I'd end up chatting in Downing Street with the Prime Minister's wife and The Queen's Maid of Honour!

I also had the privilege of meeting Nelson Mandela's grandson during a trip to South Africa. It happened after I visited a hospital where there were mothers and babies squatting on the floor because there were not enough beds. The hospital was in Nelson Mandela's name, so his grandson was invited along to the grand opening. I sat down with him and we discussed how the Hard Rock could help. Within a day, we had furnished the ward with new beds and equipment. He was a very well spoken young man and he promised to look me up if he were ever in London.

Another person who it was a pleasure to meet on a different occasion was David Beckham. I first saw him and his wife many years ago when they came into the Hard Rock and they ate downstairs. David is very polite and chatty and looks you in the eye. His wife Victoria never seems to smile in photos but she is actually very friendly in person. Apparently before she was famous she applied for a job as a waitress at the Hard Rock but for whatever reason it didn't work out. I met the Beckhams again at Hard Rock Calling. I've also met the other former members of the Spice Girls. My favorite is Mel C. She's so chatty and she will always go the extra mile if she is asked to do something for charity.

I'm never shy about approaching famous people anymore because I've found that if you are polite and treat them like normal human beings they're often only too willing to help. When I am helping to train our staff I always tell them to adopt a similar approach. I remember a few years ago at The Brit Awards in London, one of our young waitresses came running up to me with a flustered look on her face.

"Rita – I am so nervous, you've got to help me!" she cried.

"What's the matter?" I asked.

The girl explained to me that she was worried because Take That, who were the biggest pop band in the UK at the time, were sitting at her table. She was worried that she'd slip up in front of them.

"Oh for God's sake, you don't need to worry," I reassured her. "Come on, we'll do it together."

I went over to the band's table where the boys were all in deep conversation with each other, so I clapped my hands to get their attention.

"Right guys, what are we having?" I asked.

Mark Owen looked up at me in surprise.

"What part of Ireland are you from?" he asked.

I said I was from Galway and he explained that his mother was from County Mayo. After that we got along fine. When the young waitress and I brought the boys their food we discovered that they'd gone off to play football with Mick Hucknell at a mini sports area at the awards. I marched over to them and when their ball came bouncing over I kicked it to get their attention.

"Come on boys, the food is hot and it's on the table, " I told them.

They thought it was hilarious and they didn't mind being bossed about in the least. My favorite ex-member of Take That is Robbie Williams. He's got such a cheeky smile.

* * * * *

I WAS very excited about the Hard Rock Calling event that we held at the Olympic Park. I think that if I had to choose my perfect day at the Hard Rock then this would be it.

The venue was fantastic and Hard Rock laid on every possible comfort that you might need. There was even a sauna and a spa in the hospitality area. There was also a little tent with a fortuneteller who would give you a reading about your future (I was determined to see her and I hoped that I'd get a chance to have my own reading!).

Bruce Springsteen was back on the bill and when I met him before the gig he remembered me from the year before when the plug had been pulled on him at Hyde Park.

"Hiya Rita – are you still rocking?" he said.

Bruce was in great spirits and there were no hard feelings about what happened in London. He was happy to pose for a photo and I could tell he was looking forward to being on stage again.

Later that day I got a special treat in the hospitality area, which was big enough to cater for several hundred people. Among the attractions there was an old fashioned London bus that had been converted into an English tearoom. The bus was a red double–decker, decorated in Union Jack flags and pictures of the Queen. The bus was there to pay tribute to Twinings Tea, the famous old company that has been serving English tea since 1706. Stephen Twining from the Twinings family was there to greet everybody. I listened as he told me all about the history of the company while we sipped fine tea from cups made of bone china. I felt like Royalty! It struck me at that moment that I couldn't think of a better way to spend an afternoon than sipping tea in the Olympic Park. It was so calm and peaceful – yet we were in the middle of a rock festival.

Afterwards I went for a walk around the park and I saw my old friend Steven Van Zandt in the hospitality area with Chief

Billie of the Seminole Tribe. I went to join them and we had a friendly chat. While we were talking, one of the girls from the Hard Rock came over and explained that the fortuneteller in the park was now free if I wanted to go to see her for a reading.

"Go on Rita – go and see her," Steven urged me. "Then come back. I'd love to know what she says to you."

I left Steven and went to join the psychic woman at another table. I didn't know quite what to expect but I was flabbergasted by what she told me.

"I can see lots of writing in your future. I can see words on a page," she told me. "And there is a baby on the way. It might be twins or a boy, I'm not sure."

I hurried back to Steven.

"Was she right?" he asked.

"Yes maybe," I replied. "I've been talking with the Hard Rock about the possibility of doing a book."

"Wow he said – send me a copy."

"There's something else," I added.

It was a little piece of news that I had been keeping secret.

"My daughter Tara is pregnant," I told Steven.

Like I say, it was a perfect day. Tea with Mr. Twining and there was a new baby on the way . . . what more could I ask for?

22

AND FINALLY...

IT'S been a privilege to share so many great memories with you about the Hard Rock so thank you for listening. When I look back over the years I can't help but think that I've been blessed to enjoy so many happy times. The Hard Rock's unstoppable story continues to roll on through the summer of 2015. Hard Rock Calling is now a global phenomenon under its new name of Hard Rock Rising. At the time of writing I am looking forward to attending our rock festival in Barcelona, where Robbie Williams, Kings of Leon, Avicii and Lenny Kravitz will be entertaining the crowds. Meanwhile there's talk of even bigger and greater things to come in 2016, with a possible world tour for me. It's a journey that I could never have predicted during my early life in Ireland or when I first walked into the Hard Rock at the age of 29.

It's been a wonderful ride and I'm still very much involved in spreading the word about Hard Rock. As for me, I also love to spend precious time back in Galway these days where I still have many wonderful friends to share a glass of red wine with.

Meanwhile I have something else to tell you. Remember Noel, the handsome butcher's boy I fell in love with all those years ago? Well, we are back in touch and we are friends once again. It's a purely platonic relationship out of respect to our loved ones who are no longer with us. We're both happy with that. I'm delighted that our friendship has withstood the test of time and it's nice to have a man who I can meet with to share a cup of coffee.

I'm also pleased to say that I'm a very proud grandmother!

The fortuneteller was right because the child that my daughter gave birth to was a baby boy. He is my darling little angel with beautiful red hair. His name is Howard but I call him Howie. His photos take pride of place on my iPhone along with my oldest grandson, Ryan, whom I also adore. Ryan is in his teens. He loves swimming and he has a warm heart.

I love my grandchildren very much, along with my three children John (Ryan's dad), Darren and Tara. I've learned that people are the things that matter the most in life.

I recently celebrated my 74th birthday but like I said earlier in this book, when that telephone rings and it's Hard Rock on the line, then I feel like I'm aged 29 again and I'm pulling on my uniform for the first time.

I think that in my heart I'll always be 29.

THANK YOU

I would like to say thank you to the all of the following for making my journey so special...

To Galway: *the city of my birth.*

To my family: *My parents Cecelia and Martin Ryan; my children John Anthony, Darren Joseph and Tara Elizabeth Gilligan; my grandchildren Ryan and Howard; my siblings Maureen, Michael, Ann and Martina.*

To my late husband: *Tony Gilligan, may he rest in peace.*

To my special friends: *Gertie Elwood and Monica Phillips – and Frank Shields, my guest and customer for 44 years!*

To the founders of Hard Rock Cafe: *Isaac Tigrett and Peter Morton.*

To my colleagues over the years: *Prab Nallamilli, Marc Carey, Elizabeth Clotherty (RIP), Betty Grant (RIP), Steve Byrne, Maggie Byrne, Al Larmond, Angelos, Sherrie Byrne, Calum MacPherson, our CEO Hamish Dodds and the Seminole Tribe of Florida. Plus all the wonderful staff of Hard Rock Cafe worldwide... you know who you are.*

To my all my wonderful customers: *each and every one of you.*

...Love Rita x

INDEX

INDEX